LET'S TALK ABOUT

RELIGION AND MENTAL HEALTH

OTHER BOOKS IN THE
LET'S TALK ABOUT SERIES

Let's Talk about Polygamy

Let's Talk about the Book of Abraham
(coming January 2022)

For more information on the other books
in the Let's Talk About series,
visit DesBook.com/LetsTalk.

LET'S TALK ABOUT

RELIGION AND MENTAL HEALTH

DANIEL K JUDD

SALT LAKE CITY, UTAH

This book is dedicated to Elder Jeffrey R. Holland, Professor Allen E. Bergin, and Professor Richard N. Williams.

© 2021 Daniel K Judd

All rights reserved. No part of this book may be reproduced in any form or by any means without permission in writing from the publisher, Deseret Book Company, at permissions@deseretbook.com. This work is not an official publication of The Church of Jesus Christ of Latter-day Saints. The views expressed herein are the responsibility of the author and do not necessarily represent the position of the Church, of Brigham Young University, or of Deseret Book Company.

DESERET BOOK is a registered trademark of Deseret Book Company.

Visit us at deseretbook.com

Library of Congress Cataloging-in-Publication Data
Names: Judd, Daniel K, author.
Title: Let's talk about religion and mental health / Daniel K Judd.
Description: Salt Lake City, Utah : Deseret Book, [2021] | Series:
    Let's talk about | Includes bibliographical references and index. |
    Summary: "Latter-day Saint author Daniel K Judd discusses mental
    health in the context of believing Latter-day Saint doctrine and
    policy"—Provided by publisher.
Identifiers: LCCN 2021016453 | ISBN 9781629728254 (paperback)
Subjects: LCSH: Mental health—Religious aspects—The Church
    of Jesus Christ of Latter-day Saints. | Mental health—Religious
    aspects—Mormon Church. | Mormons—Mental health.
Classification: LCC BX8643.M45 J83 2021 | DDC 261.5/61—dc23
LC record available at https://lccn.loc.gov/2021016453

Printed in the United States of America
PubLitho, Draper, UT

10 9 8 7 6 5 4 3 2 1

CONTENTS

Acknowledgments vii

Introduction 1

1. Depression, Sickness, Sorrow, and the
   Gospel of Jesus Christ 12

2. Anxiety and the Grace of Jesus Christ 34

3. Psychotic Disorders, Self-Deception, and
   Personal Revelation 52

4. Parents, Children, and Mental Health 65

5. Healing the Broken Brain 75

6. Healing the Broken Heart 92

Conclusion 110

Further Reading 115

Notes 118

Index 131

ACKNOWLEDGMENTS

My introduction to the study of the relationship of religion and mental health began when I read the research and writing of Professor Allen E. Bergin. Allen later became an important mentor and good friend. Professor C. Terry Warner and Professor Richard N. Williams have also been cherished friends and trusted mentors. These three remarkable scholars and friends see the world in different ways, but they share an unwavering commitment to Jesus Christ and to the restored gospel.

Many friends and colleagues at Brigham Young University have contributed to the publication of this manuscript. I especially want to thank Lori Soza, my executive assistant, and my research assistant, Brianna Bartlett Smith, for their able work. The staff of the Harold B. Lee Library has also been especially helpful, especially given the added burden of providing resources amid a worldwide pandemic.

Professor Robert L. Millet, Professor P. Scott Richards, Professor James S. Jacobs, Professor Camille Fronk Olson, Sister Virginia Hinckley Pearce Cowley, Brother Jacob Daniel Judd, and three anonymous reviewers all offered exceptionally helpful reviews.

I also want to thank all of those at Deseret Book who have made this publication possible. Special thanks to Lisa Brown Roper, Alison Palmer, Laurel Christensen Day, Sheri L. Dew, Richard Erickson, Emily Remington, Rachael Ward, and the members of Deseret Book's brilliant review board.

ACKNOWLEDGMENTS

I am grateful to my courageous wife, Kaye; our four remarkable children—Jake, Jessi, Rachel, and Adam; our sons- and daughters-in-law; and our grandchildren. Thank you for your love and support.

INTRODUCTION

> "I am . . . subject to all manner of
> infirmities in body and mind."
> —*Mosiah 2:11*

Let's Talk about Religion and Mental Health is a brief introduction to a sobering subject that is becoming a more significant part of the lives of individuals, families, and communities among "every nation, kindred, tongue and people" (1 Ne. 19:17) than ever before. Over the last several years, media accounts and scholarly journals alike report an increase in a wide range of mental and emotional problems, including anxiety and depression. The World Health Organization recently stated, "Globally, more than 300 million people of all ages suffer from depression. . . . The burden of depression and other mental health conditions is on the rise globally."[1] Dramatic increases in drug addiction and suicide among people of all ages have also been reported.[2]

Chemical imbalances, the judgments of God, poor parenting, poverty, social isolation, social media, abusive relationships, food additives, nutrition, the environment, education, and geographic elevation are among the explanations that have been given for the presence of mental illness. In my experience, however, the reasons for the psychological problems we face and the cures we seek aren't always as easy to identify as some would have us believe. Progress is being made, but identifying the origins and cures of mental and emotional disorders has been, and continues to be, one of the great challenges facing the human family.

The chapters that follow include possible reasons for the reported increases in mental and emotional challenges and how we can meaningfully address these concerns in our own lives and in the lives of those we love and serve. One of the unique contributions of this particular publication is its focus on assisting people of faith, specifically those who are members of The Church of Jesus Christ of Latter-day Saints, in identifying and navigating these difficult challenges.

This book is based on the doctrinal foundation that God is our Father, He loves us, and because we are "subject to all manner of infirmities in body and mind" (Mosiah 2:11), He has provided the means to "heal all manner of sickness and all manner of disease" (Matt. 10:1). Through the gift of the redemptive sacrifice of Jesus Christ; the guidance provided through revelation to prophets; the contributions of capable counselors, physicians, scientists, leaders, and teachers; and our own faithfulness, humility, and diligence, we can find the answers and peace we seek.

My personal study of the relationship between religion and mental health has been a significant part of my personal, professional, and pastoral journey for the past forty years. Being trained as a psychologist, serving in the Church at local and general levels, and working as a university professor have provided me with unique perspectives on the challenges we face. Most importantly, these experiences have strengthened my testimony of Jesus Christ and of the depth and power of the restored gospel, and have increased my appreciation for the blessings of academic research and clinical practice. While there are many answers yet to be discovered concerning the complexities of the relationships of religion and mental health, there is much that has been revealed that can assist us in our individual and collective journeys.

My personal experience with religion and mental health began as a young man growing up in Kanab, Utah, in the early 1970s. Even though I had a supportive family and good friends, my feelings of anxiety and despair were a heavy burden. I didn't have access to the healthcare resources that are available today, but it was during these difficult days that I found answers to many of my personal questions and concerns. I learned of my inability to overcome my physical afflictions and emotional burdens alone, which allowed me to discover the love of God; the merits, mercy, and grace of Jesus Christ; and a thirst for knowledge, both sacred and secular.

Religion, Mental Health, and the Latter-day Saints

During graduate school I began what has become a lifelong study of the relationships between religious belief and practice and mental health. While I have sifted through thousands of publications—including media reports, personal accounts, and book-length manuscripts—I have spent most of my career studying the doctrinal teachings of ancient and modern prophets, searching scholarly journals, and working with individuals and families in educational, clinical, and pastoral settings. I have discovered, with few exceptions, that scholarly research generally supports the conclusion that religious belief, and most especially personal religious devotion, contributes to mental health, marital strength, and family stability.[3]

Even though studies reveal that faithful members of The Church of Jesus Christ of Latter-day Saints do suffer with mental illness and emotional disturbance, research findings on mental health are especially favorable for Church members who are striving to live the covenants they have made.[4] Though most studies on Latter-day Saints focus on specific mental health measures, studies describing the overall mental and emotional challenges of those in the United States can be applied to Latter-day Saints in general. The following table lists the average percentages of adults (eighteen and older) and adolescents (twelve through seventeen) in the United States who reported symptoms of various mental disorders. It applies these percentages to a hypothetical stake and ward of The Church of Jesus Christ of Latter-day Saints. The "statistical" stake I have created for this illustration is based on statistical averages and has a membership of 2,500 people composing seven wards, with an average of 350 men, women, and children in each unit.

Classification of Mental Illness[5]	United States	Stake	Ward
Adults			
Symptoms of Major Depression	7.1%	123	17
Symptoms of Anxiety	19.1%	330	46
Symptoms of Post-Traumatic Stress	3.6%	62	9
Symptoms of Obsessive Compulsive Disorder (OCD)	1.2%	21	3
Symptoms of Schizophrenia	0.64%	11	1
Youth			
Symptoms of Major Depression	13.3%	103	15
Eating Disorders	2.7%	21	3
Attention Deficit Hyperactivity	11.0%	85	12

Though the numbers in the last two columns are hypothetical and shouldn't be taken literally, the comparison provides an idea of how prevalent the symptoms of mental illness are among our friends and neighbors.

The overall body of research from the early part of the twentieth century to the present is hopeful. Research supports the conclusion that Latter-day Saints who are striving to live their lives consistent with the teachings of the Savior and His servants experience greater well-being, increased marital and family stability, less delinquency, less depression, less anxiety, and less substance abuse than many of those who are not.[6]

Many, if not most, of those who read this book will join me in sharing faith in God and confidence in His servants. With that stated, this book includes multiple examples of how misunderstanding and misapplying the doctrine, principles, practices, and beliefs of the restored gospel can contribute to emotional and mental instability. As much as I oppose the uninformed arguments of the critics of religion in general and antagonists of the Church of Jesus Christ in particular, there are lessons to be learned from some of their observations.

The General Handbook of Instructions states: "In today's world, information is easy to access and share. This can be a great blessing for those seeking to be educated and informed. However, many sources of information are unreliable and do not edify. . . . Members of the Church should seek out and share only credible, reliable, and factual sources of information. They should avoid sources that are speculative or founded on rumor."[7] The pages that follow reference credible and reliable sources and provide several examples of how both religious teachings and scientific findings have been misunderstood and how we can avoid allowing these distortions to become a part of our lives. Recommendations are also included to help readers identify and understand "sound doctrine" (1 Tim. 1:10) and recognize clinical research that can be trusted, understood, and appropriately applied.[8]

Creation, Fall, and Atonement

The doctrinal pattern of the *Creation* of the world and all humankind, the *Fall* of Adam and Eve, and the *Atonement* of Jesus Christ underlies the message of this book. In addition to representing actual historical events, these divine doctrines can also be understood as metaphorical experiences. Most of us have had "Garden of Eden" experiences where, in an idyllic sense, "the grass was green, the water was clear, and the sky was blue," only to find later that these experiences were not as wonderful as we had originally hoped they would be. Some of these experiences are faith shaking—sobering reminders of the fallen world in which we live.

The "good news" is that the Atonement of Jesus Christ reconciles the hopeful expectations of the Creation with the oftentimes disappointing and even tragic realities of the Fall. The necessity of working through the complexities of life is inherent in the doctrine of the "fortunate fall" of Adam and Eve (see 2 Ne. 2), one of the many doctrines that is unique to the restored gospel of Jesus Christ. Mortality, by divine design, is intended to be difficult. Understanding the significance of the doctrinal trilogy of our divine creation, the Fall of Adam and Eve (and the fall of you and me), and the Atonement of Jesus Christ provides meaning and healing for every aspect of our lives, including the sobering realities of physical and mental illness, and underscores the reality of the Savior's promise "I will heal thee of thy wounds" (Jer. 30:17).[9] We must also remember that the fullness of the blessings we seek through the Atonement of Christ will not be realized until after we are resurrected (see Alma 11:44).

"All Truth Is Part of the Gospel of Jesus Christ"

Throughout this book I write about mental and emotional problems from the perspectives of both faith and reason. Much of my focus on *faith* includes the teachings of the Savior and His servants, and my attention to *reason* is informed by the writings of scholars and clinicians; I believe our Heavenly Father wants us to understand and to exercise *both* faith and reason as companion principles in our pursuit of truth and peace (see D&C 8:20). Authentic faith in God includes genuine reason, and genuine reason includes authentic faith. President Russell M. Nelson recently affirmed: "There is no conflict between science and religion. Conflict only arises from an incomplete knowledge of either science or religion or both. . . . All truth is part of the gospel of Jesus Christ. Whether truth comes from a scientific laboratory or by revelation from the Lord, it is compatible."[10]

Attempting to focus on faith without reason, or reason

without faith, can contribute to the mental and emotional problems we face. An imbalance in understanding these two principles can negatively affect our decisions about engaging in therapy, identifying a therapist, using psychiatric medications, helping family and friends with mental health concerns, and exercising faith in God during personal and family crises. Decisions so significant require both reasoned and faithful inquiry. As the Lord taught Oliver Cowdery, "I will tell you in your mind and your heart, by the Holy Ghost, which shall come upon you and which shall dwell in your heart. . . . This is the spirit of revelation" (D&C 8:2–3). President Nelson taught, "Good inspiration is based upon good information." He continued, "In coming days, it will not be possible to survive spiritually without the guiding, directing, comforting, and constant influence of the Holy Ghost. My beloved brothers and sisters, I plead with you to increase your spiritual capacity to receive revelation."[11]

Truth and Counterfeit

In addition to helping readers better understand the inspired relationship between faith and reason in the context of religion and mental health, the pages that follow provide examples of different ways these principles can be harmonized and also distorted. Just as there are doctrinal pairs of inspired principles such as faith and reason, justice and mercy, confidence and meekness, grace and works, etc., there are counterfeit "pairs of opposites" that are also important to understand and to avoid. C. S. Lewis (1898–1963) once observed that the devil "always sends errors into the world in pairs—pairs of opposites. And he always encourages us to spend a lot of time thinking which is the worse. You see why, of course? He relies on your extra dislike of the one error to draw you gradually into the opposite one. But do not let us be fooled. We have to keep our eyes on the goal and go straight through between both errors."[12]

President Ezra Taft Benson (1899–1994) once said, "Whenever the God of heaven reveals His gospel to mankind,

Satan, the archenemy to Christ, introduces a counterfeit."[13] Because distorted ideas (counterfeits) can be found in the writings of science as well as in religious belief and practice, I believe it is vital for us to learn how to discern truth from error as we attempt to understand the relationship between religion and mental health.

When a doctrine or principle of truth is distorted or misinterpreted beyond its inspired meaning or intended application, we run the risk of reaping unintended consequences. The Prophet Joseph Smith once taught: "The human family are very apt to run to extremes, especially in religious matters."[14] President Boyd K. Packer similarly taught, "A virtue when pressed to the extreme may turn into a vice. Unreasonable devotion to an ideal, without considering the practical application of it, ruins the ideal itself."[15] The Book of Mormon prophet Jacob used the phrase "looking beyond the mark" (Jacob 4:14) to describe this same process by which the ancient Israelites rejected Jesus Christ as the Messiah. They looked "beyond" the mortal Jesus for a mystical messiah or a political liberator to deliver them in a manner fitting their own biases and expectations. Like our ancient brothers and sisters, we too can "look beyond the mark" and by so doing miss finding the Savior and receiving the answers we are seeking.

One of the methods or "tools" I have found helpful in working though the complex issues found in the fallen world was originally inspired by the words of the Prophet Joseph Smith when he quoted the following from an unknown source: "By proving contrarieties, truth is made manifest."[16] In other words, as we faithfully and diligently study what appear to be contradictory principles and practices, we can come to a knowledge of "things as they really are, and of things as they really will be" (Jacob 4:13).

Learning to understand doctrinal, philosophical, and psychological contrasts, counterfeits, and paradoxes can help us as we work through complex issues. While the principles of faith and reason, for example, are central to understanding the relationship of religion and mental health and can be harmonized with one another, each principle can also be distorted and misapplied. Faith can be distorted into a form of mindless mysticism or extreme fundamentalism. Reason can also become distorted into a faithless intellectualism or dogmatic scientism, devoid of God's inspiration. While the following illustration (one of several included throughout the book) can be used to show an infinite number of contrasts between truth and untruth, I will use the contrast between faith and reason to illustrate what it means to engage in "proving contrarieties," as taught by the Prophet Joseph, to help us understand truth and counterfeit:

The principles of *faith* and *reason* at the center of the diagram are complementary and mutually sustaining and help define one another. These doctrinal principles are perfectly expressed in the character of Christ and are intended to lead us to and help us become like Him. The philosophies of *mysticism* and *scientism*, on the extreme ends of the continuum, are counterfeits of faith and reason and represent distortions we need to learn to identify and avoid.

When the principle of *faith in God* is taken to an extreme, it becomes a form of *mysticism*, which can be defined as an exclusive reliance on emotion or even magic and is often accompanied by a "disparagement of reason."[17] For example, some individuals respond to the threat of sickness by thinking and saying things like, "We do not need to take precautions to protect ourselves from sickness or injury; God will protect us." God can and does intervene in such crises, but this kind of mystical thinking can be destructive to individuals and families and is an example of the distorted beliefs that can lead to sickness and death, and in some cases, to a loss of faith in God. Such an argument can also be a part of what causes people to question the goodness of God, when sickness and death come as a result of mystical thoughts and unwise actions. This same pattern of distorted thinking can be found in the idea that mental illness is caused by sin. Despair can come from iniquity (see Moro. 10:22), but as will be discussed in later chapters, the Savior taught that our "Father which is in heaven . . . sendeth rain on the just and on the unjust" (Matt. 5:45). Adversity is no respecter of persons.

Elder David A. Bednar taught, "Faithfulness is not foolishness or fanaticism. Rather, it is trusting and placing our confidence in Jesus Christ as our Savior, on His name, and in His promises."[18] Faith in Christ includes submission to Him, to His will, to His teachings, and to the counsel He provides through His servants, and from personal revelation. We can also learn to identify and to exercise faith in the truth God reveals through inspired philosophers, teachers, scientists, and clinicians.

The importance of *reason* is illustrated in the Lord's counsel: "Let us *reason* together, that ye may understand" (D&C 50:10; emphasis added). However, individuals who take reason to an extreme are often deceived by distorted thinking described by the term *scientism*. Those who adhere to the philosophy of scientism base their arguments on the proposition that "only science is capable of producing real knowledge."[19] The atheist philosopher Bertrand Russell (1872–1970) once described scientism as "whatever knowledge is attainable, must be attained by scientific methods; and what science cannot discover, mankind cannot know."[20] Professor Russell's words echo the argument made by the Book of Mormon anti-Christ Korihor, who stated: "Behold, ye cannot know of things which ye do not see" (Alma 30:15).

Like the counterfeit currency that has been created by a capable criminal, a counterfeit doctrine crafted by the evil one can be made to appear genuine to the untrained heart and mind. President Joseph F. Smith once taught: "Satan is a skillful imitator, and as genuine gospel truth is given the world in ever-increasing abundance, so he spreads the counterfeit coin of false doctrine. Beware of his spurious currency, it will purchase for you nothing but disappointment, misery and spiritual death."[21] Comparisons between truth and counterfeit will be used throughout the book to assist in discussing the complexity and simplicity of the relationship between mental health and religion.

Let's Talk about Religion and Mental Health is not intended to be a diagnostic tool or to provide personal counsel but is an introduction and educational resource. In addition to providing scriptural and doctrinal teachings, clinical and pastoral examples, and relevant research findings, this book includes practical tools and suggestions for additional reading to help the reader better understand complex issues, make informed decisions, and use their God-given gifts to address the problems they face. Of special note, the chapters that follow describe the mental and emotional afflictions faced by individuals whose lives are documented in scripture and in the history of the Church. "Now all these things happened unto them for ensamples," the Apostle Paul explained, "and they are written for our admonition" (1 Cor. 10:11).

Our Heavenly Parents love Their children and desire for us to become like Them. Jesus Christ, the Son of God, was sent to earth to teach us His gospel, atone for our sins, be resurrected, and through His grace provide us with the strength to manage and, in many cases, overcome the obstacles we are powerless to overcome on our own—including mental illness and emotional distress.

CHAPTER 1

DEPRESSION, SICKNESS, SORROW, AND THE GOSPEL OF JESUS CHRIST

> "If ye have no hope ye must needs be in despair."
> —*Moroni 10:22*

During the Saturday afternoon session of the October 2013 general conference, Elder Jeffrey R. Holland shared what has become a "balm in Gilead" (Jer. 8:22) for many Latter-day Saints troubled with mental and emotional illness. In his address, entitled "Like a Broken Vessel," Elder Holland acknowledged the distinction between being "downhearted," experiencing "discouraging moments," and suffering from "depression."

Elder Holland also included a candid description of his own personal experience with the "dark night of the mind and spirit": "At one point . . . when financial fears collided with staggering fatigue, I took a psychic blow that was as unanticipated as it was real. With the grace of God and the love of my family, I kept functioning and kept working, but even after all these years I continue to feel a deep sympathy for others more chronically or more deeply afflicted with such gloom than I was."[1]

Having a member of the Quorum of the Twelve specifically mention "major depressive disorder," "neuroses and psychoses . . . genetic predispositions and chromosome defects . . . bipolarity, paranoia, and schizophrenia" in a general conference address was unprecedented. Elder Holland's acknowledgment of these psychiatric disorders and his own experience with emotional suffering have helped many Latter-day Saints better understand the Savior's words (mentioned earlier) "For he [God] maketh his sun to rise on the evil and on the good, and sendeth rain on the just and on the unjust" (Matt. 5:45). Elder Holland's personal account illustrates that the Lord allows even one of the most faithful among us—even one of the Lord's Apostles—to experience mental distress and emotional affliction.

The history of the Lord's covenant people, both ancient and modern, includes many examples of individuals who have experienced mental and emotional suffering. The following examples from the life of President George Albert Smith (1870–1951), the eighth president of The Church of Jesus Christ of Latter-day Saints; and King David (1040–970 BC), the shepherd boy who became the King of Israel, illustrate that depression has unique expressions in the lives of a wide range of individuals, families, and communities.

President George Albert Smith

While it is difficult, and in some cases unethical, for a mental health professional to make a clinical diagnosis of someone without having met with him or her face-to-face, it is well established that President George Albert Smith suffered from multiple physical and mental health problems during his lifetime, including what may have been "clinical depression." Many of the symptoms described by President Smith in his own writings and by those closely associated with him are consistent with many of the clinical criteria mental health professionals refer to as "major depressive disorder."[2]

When thirty-three-year-old George Albert Smith was sustained as an apostle on October 8, 1903, his father, Elder John Henry Smith—also an apostle—expressed concern for his son's health and stated, "He's not healthy. He won't last long."[3] Six years after his call to the Quorum of the Twelve Apostles, Elder George Albert Smith received the following letter from his uncle Dr. Heber J. Sears, a physician practicing in Chicago,

Illinois. Dr. Sears's letter provides insight into some of the details of the challenges faced by the young apostle:

> April 12, 1909
> My Dear Nephew,
>
> A letter from your Mother brings the sad intelligence that you are down with nervous prostration. I take no satisfaction in saying "I told you so" but I do wish that I could say something that could bring you to a realization of the danger you are in. For years I have seen the necessity of a period of complete relaxation and have endeavored to warn you of the consequences that are sure to follow such a prolonged tension. Nature is now giving you a warning which you will do well to take. When the nervous system is once broken down the patient is too often a wreck for life. No class of diseases resist so stubbornly the efforts of the physician as nervous diseases. In fact, there is but little hope after they reach a certain stage. Their manifestations cover a wide range—from slight nervous instability to insanity. I need but call your attention to the number of good people who have gone insane in your own locality and in the same field of usefulness that your own efforts are directed in. Insanity is largely on the increase as statistics will show. And let me whisper a very significant fact in your ear—it is only a step from nervous prostration to insanity. For Heaven's sake George—"sidestep" or step backward not forward. Cheat the asylum of a victim. Dump your responsibility for a while before the hearse dumps your bones.
>
> Once more I will make the plea. If you are doing all this for humanity stay with humanity as long as you can and administer the [medicine] in broken doses. If the church requires your life, give it to The Church in a thinner layer spread over 30 or 40 more years instead of 3 to 5. Could you not do more good in this way?
>
> There are more ways of keeping the word of wisdom than by abstaining from tea, coffee, [and] beer. You are an apostle. While I have only one foot in the church yet in

my opinion, I keep the Word of Wisdom better than you do. Should there be any dispute on this point I would offer in evidence a body of 48 years young, in a splendid state of preservation—free from disease—and capable of great endurance.

Now George! Wake up. We can't afford to lose you. Give the "other fellows" an inning while you drink lemonade in the shade. Call "Casey to the bat" and you watch the game while the others run the bases for a while. Or you'll be hauled off in the ambulance before the game is half over.

Give our best love to your family and accept the same for yourself. With a strong hope that you will be good to yourself. I remain,

Your affectionate Uncle,

H J Sears[4]

Dr. Sears used the term "nervous prostration" to describe and diagnose Elder Smith's malady. In 1844, Dr. Roberts Bartholow defined nervous prostration as "a state of debility, in which nervous derangements predominate. A man actively engaged in business or in public life presently finds himself unequal to his daily tasks; he suffers odd sensations in his head; his digestion is disordered; he is weak; wakefulness, mental depression, and a thousand and one new sensations of strange character and fearful portent are superadded."[5]

Elder Smith was called as an apostle at thirty-three and as President of the Church when he was seventy-five. He died at age eighty-one, having faithfully served as an apostle for nearly forty-eight years. President Smith's journals indicate that he suffered most every day of his adult life, to a greater or lesser degree, from physical affliction and mental distress. The challenges President Smith faced and the afflictions he endured were certainly a part of what identified him as one of "the noble and great ones who were chosen in the beginning to be rulers in the Church of God" (D&C 138:55).

In a letter dated April 9, 1909, the newly called apostle's father, President John Henry Smith, who had been sustained as second counselor in the First Presidency at the general conference the year his son was called to the Quorum of the Twelve, wrote the following words of encouragement and prophecy, even though he had serious concerns about his son's health: "Keep up good fortitude and good faith; don't waiver in your determination to live. The bitter experience through which you are going is but designed for your purification and uplifting and qualification for an extended life work."[6] The faith and courage of President George Albert Smith and the support of his wife, family, and fellow apostles are important examples of individuals who pressed forward, meeting personal, familial, ecclesiastical, and professional responsibilities, even while addressing the challenges of serious mental and physical illness.

President Smith's story also introduces several dimensions of dealing with depression that can be helpful in understanding what has been described by many of the leaders of the early Christian church as "the noonday demon," alluded to in Psalm 91:6.[7] Some of the lessons we learn from President Smith's experiences with depression include:

1. Individuals who have faith in God and earnestly strive to keep His commandments can experience depression. Personal righteousness doesn't always prevent or cure mental and emotional suffering.
2. Depression is often found in association with serious and chronic physical illness.
3. Depression, to greater and lesser degrees, may be a burden with which some people are afflicted for the duration of their mortal lives.
4. Depression doesn't necessarily prevent a person from accomplishing his or her life's mission and from living a meaningful and rewarding life.
5. Depression can be an experience God allows for the qualification and purification of those who suffer.

DEPRESSION, SICKNESS, SORROW, AND THE GOSPEL

Depression and Sorrow

President Smith's experiences also illustrate the qualitative differences between depression and sorrow. In a letter to a stake president, Ralph E. Wooley, President Smith wrote: "Even when things are normal my nerves are not very strong and when I see other people in sorrow or depressed I am easily affected."[8] Speaking of himself, President Smith once told a friend that "he lacked the prowess to be an athlete, that he was too homely to win popular favor, and that his weak eyes prevented him from becoming a scholar, but he could excel in human kindness. So, he made kindness his specialty."[9] President Smith's writings (and those who wrote about him) reveal his deep sensitivity and compassion for others. His life embodied the covenant disciples of Jesus Christ make "to mourn with those that mourn" (Mosiah 18:9). From his writings, it is clear that President Smith sought out and followed the counsel of his physicians for the treatment of *depression*, but his writings also reveal that he understood and embraced *sorrow* and *sadness* in his own life and the lives of others, believing physical and emotional afflictions to be a necessary part of the human condition.

The scriptural phrase "Jesus wept" (John 11:35) succinctly describes the sorrow Jesus expressed at the death of Lazarus and the mourning of his sisters, Mary and Martha. From my own professional and ecclesiastical experience, it isn't unusual for someone to apologize for their tears as we discuss personal issues that are painful. In my attempts to comfort them, I often respond, "No need to apologize. 'Jesus wept,' and He was and is a perfect being." It is important to understand that sorrow, sadness, and tears are attributes of God—characteristics to be emulated and embraced and not pathologized. Dr. Allen Frances, a psychiatrist and former chairman of the Department of Psychiatry at Duke University School of Medicine, recently stated:

> Sadness should not be synonymous with sickness. There is no diagnosis for every disappointment or a pill

for every problem. Life's difficulties—divorce, illness, job loss, financial troubles, interpersonal conflicts—can't be legislated away. And our natural reactions to them—sadness, dissatisfaction, and discouragement—shouldn't all be medicalized as mental disorder or treated with a pill. . . . Our capacity to feel emotional pain has great adaptive value equivalent in its purpose to physical pain—a signal that something has gone wrong. We can't convert all emotional pain into mental disorder without radically changing who we are, dulling the palette of our experience.[10]

Dr. Frances is one of a growing number of mental health professionals who believe that at least some of the dramatic increases in the incidences of depression in the last several decades can be explained by the conflation of the sorrow experienced by most everyone and the clinical depression experienced by others. Professors Allan Horwitz and Jerome Wakefield explain: "We argue that the recent explosion of . . . depressive disorder . . . is largely a product of conflating the two conceptually distinct categories of normal sadness and depressive disorder and thus classifying many instances of normal sadness as mental disorders."[11]

Sorrow and sadness are normal responses to loss—often the loss of someone or something we love. These experiences, while deeply painful, are often temporary, rarely disabling, and often instructive and are to be embraced. Comparatively, depression often begins as sadness or sorrow but then evolves into something much more severe, becoming pervasive, long-term, and debilitating—a condition to be addressed and hopefully overcome. The American Psychological Association (APA) defines depression as "a negative [emotional] state, ranging from unhappiness and discontent to an extreme feeling of sadness, pessimism, and despondency, that interferes with daily life."[12] The following diagram illustrates the contrasts between depression and sorrow, joy and mania:

DEPRESSION, SICKNESS, SORROW, AND THE GOSPEL

	SORROW	JOY	
DEPRESSION			MANIA

Much of the sorrow we experience and the tears we shed are expressions of the attributes of God and evidence that we are His children. The prophet Lehi taught that if Adam and Eve had not partaken of the fruit of the tree of knowledge of good and evil and remained in the Garden of Eden, they would have had "no joy, *for they knew no misery*" (2 Ne. 2:23; emphasis added). Joy and sorrow are doctrinally and personally linked, help define one another, and are central to the very purpose of our mortal journey (see 2 Ne. 2:24–25).

Similar to the contrast between depression and sorrow, psychologists also make an important distinction between joy and mania. Mania has been defined as "a state of excitement, overactivity . . . often accompanied by overoptimism, grandiosity, or impaired judgment."[13] In contrast, the APA defines joy as "a feeling of extreme gladness, delight, or exultation of the spirit arising from a sense of well-being or satisfaction."[14] President Russell M. Nelson taught: "Each of us has likely had times when distress, anguish, and despair almost consumed us. Yet we are here to have joy? Yes! The answer is a resounding yes."[15]

A God of Body, Parts, and Emotions

The Pearl of Great Price includes a remarkable exchange between the prophet Enoch and God concerning His sorrow and tears over the wickedness of His children. The account reads in part as follows: "And it came to pass that the God of heaven looked upon the residue of the people, and he wept; and Enoch bore record of it, saying: *How is it that the heavens weep, and shed forth their tears as the rain upon the mountains?* And Enoch said unto the Lord: *How is it that thou canst weep*, seeing thou art holy, and from all eternity to all eternity?" (Moses 7:28–29; emphasis added).

In other words, Enoch is saying, "You are the God of the

universe—how can *You* cry?" The Lord's response to Enoch is a tender representation of the sorrow and love He feels for His children: "The Lord said unto Enoch: Behold these thy brethren; they are the workmanship of mine own hands, and I gave unto them their knowledge, in the day I created them; and in the Garden of Eden, gave I unto man his agency; and unto thy brethren have I said, and also given commandment, that they should love one another, and that they should choose me, their Father; but behold, they are without affection, and they hate their own blood" (Moses 7:32–33).

The depth of depression associated with major depressive disorder can include sorrow, but clinical depression is often a different experience than the sadness we experience at the death or prolonged absence of a loved one, the sickness of a family member or friend, a shattered dream or disappointment, the loss of a job, or even the "godly sorrow" (2 Cor. 7:10) that comes with sin and repentance. Sadness and sorrow are most often a normal and temporary response to loss, but depression is often a psychological disorder that is "recurring and disruptive"[16] and has no clearly defined cause.

Joy and sorrow are both emotions to be experienced and embraced in mortality and throughout eternity. Depression and mania are experiences to be identified, understood, learned from, and eventually overcome, either in this life or the next. John the Revelator wrote that the day will come when "God shall wipe away all tears from their eyes; and there shall be no more death, neither sorrow, nor crying, neither shall there be any more pain: for the former things are passed away" (Rev. 21:4; see also Rev. 7:17; Isa. 25:8).

King David

The title of Elder Holland's address "Like a Broken Vessel" (mentioned earlier) is originally found in the text of Psalm 31—a song of lament written by King David in one of his many descriptions of his own feelings of despair and brokenness: "For my life is spent with grief, and my years with sighing: my strength faileth because of mine iniquity, and my bones are consumed. I was a reproach among all mine enemies, but especially among my neighbours, and a fear to mine acquaintance: they that did see me without fled from me. I am forgotten as a dead man out of mind: *I am like a broken vessel*" (Ps. 31:10–12; emphasis added).

The phrase "I am like a broken vessel" is particularly descriptive of the feelings of those who suffer with depression. These individuals often describe their lives as once having meaning and purpose, but their experience with depression includes feeling useless and unwanted. "Feelings of worthlessness" is one of several formal diagnostic criteria (listed in the following table) used by mental health professionals to diagnose major depressive disorder.[17]

Scriptural accounts lack sufficient detail to provide a definitive diagnosis, but many of the symptoms included in the scriptural narrative of King David are credible indicators that he suffered with serious psychological distress. The following table illustrates the diagnostic criteria, symptoms, and scriptural references that indicate David may very well have suffered with depression:[18]

Diagnostic Criteria	David's Symptoms	Scriptural References
Depressed mood	Mourning, sorrow, weeping	Psalms 6:6–7; 13:2; 31:10; 38:6–9
Diminished pleasure	Sorrow in his heart daily	Psalm 13:3
Weight loss or gain	Doesn't eat, bones cling to flesh, weak from constant fasting	Psalms 102:4–5; 109:24
Insomnia or hypersomnia	Crying at night, can't sleep	Psalms 6:6; 22:2; 102:7; 2 Sam. 11:2
Physical agitation	Trembling, periods of being deaf and dumb	Psalms 38:13–14; 55:5

Diagnostic Criteria	David's Symptoms	Scriptural References
Fatigue	Strength dried up, heart withered	Psalms 22:14–15; 31:10; 32:4; 38:10; 102:4
Feelings of worthlessness	Feeling like a worm, like no one cares, like a broken vessel	Psalms 22:6; 31:12–13; 69:12
Diminished ability to think	Did not go to battle, indecisive	2 Samuel 11:1; 13:2; 18:5; 19:1–7; 1 Kings 1:6
Recurrent thoughts of death	Dust of death, terrors of death	Psalms 22:15; 55:4

One scholar described David as "a man of many talents—a shepherd, musician, poet, warrior, politician, administrator—but he is most prominent as the king par excellence, as the standard for all later kings, and a messianic symbol."[19] Scripturally, the young David was described as having "a beautiful countenance" (1 Sam. 16:12). In the Doctrine and Covenants we learn that because he committed adultery with Bathsheba and arranged for the death of her husband, Uriah, David "hath fallen from his exaltation" (D&C 132:39) and will not enjoy the supernal blessings that might have been his had he remained faithful.

Despite rising from obscurity to be one of the greatest kings in the history of Israel and "a man after [God's] own heart" (1 Sam. 13:14), David's personal life was complicated, full of contentious relationships—and even tragic. The accounts of David's abusive and adulterous relationship with Bathsheba and his complicity in the death of Uriah (see 2 Sam. 11–12) are nearly as well-known as his defeat of Goliath (see 1 Sam. 17–18).

As sensitive as it is to acknowledge the relationship between sin and psychological suffering, David's life clearly illustrates the Book of Mormon prophet Moroni's words "Despair cometh because of iniquity" (Moro. 10:22). David's sins appear to have been a part of the tragic events his family experienced—including sexual abuse, conspiracy, revenge, and murder—and a significant part of what led to his feelings of despair. The prophet Nathan confronted David for his sins and prophesied: "Now therefore the sword shall never depart from thine house; because thou hast despised me, and hast taken the wife of Uriah the Hittite to be thy wife. Thus saith the Lord, Behold, I will raise up evil against thee out of thine own house" (2 Sam. 12:10–11).

Depression, Sin, and the Atonement of Jesus Christ

David's sins may not have been the singular source of his mental and emotional afflictions, but they were clearly a part. President Boyd K. Packer (1924–2015) once taught: "We know that some anxiety and depression is caused by physical disorders, but much . . . of it is not a pain of the body but of the spirit. Spiritual pain resulting from guilt can be replaced with peace of mind."[20] To disregard the influences sin and transgression may have on mental health could, in some cases, be what distracts us from understanding the very solutions we are seeking.

The opinions of many mental health professionals are polarized regarding the relationship between sin and mental illness. Psychologist Dr. Albert Ellis, one of the founders of modern psychotherapy, stated, "I . . . stoutly uphold the thesis that there is *no place whatever* for the concept of sin in psychotherapy."[21] On the other hand, Dr. Jay E. Adams, the founder of the Christian Counseling and Education Association, has stated that the "*ultimate cause*" of the ills in our society, including most instances of mental illness, "is sin."[22] These opinions represent extreme perspectives, neither of which is consistent with the fullness of the gospel expressed in the doctrines and practices of The Church of Jesus Christ of Latter-day Saints.

Sin was once believed to be the origin of much of the adversity and affliction experienced by humankind, but during the last few decades there has been a significant shift from *sin* to *sickness* as being the primary explanation. The philosophical, cultural, and therapeutic shift in emphasis from sin to sickness is a recent phenomenon, but the discussion has ancient origins. Note the following dialogue between the Savior and His servants concerning the reasons for a man's physical blindness: "And as Jesus passed by, he saw a man which was blind from his birth. And his disciples asked him, saying, Master, who did sin, this man, or his parents, that he was born blind? Jesus answered, Neither hath this man sinned, nor his parents: but that the works of God should be made manifest in him" (John 9:1–3).

The most persuasive example that depression and sorrow are not always the result of sin or transgression is the life of Jesus Christ. The Savior suffered in every way, including deep sorrow, but he was never guilty of sin. Elder Holland clearly cautioned against correlating sin with sickness when he stated, "There should be no more shame in acknowledging [mental illness] than in acknowledging a battle with high blood pressure or the sudden appearance of a malignant tumor."[23] However, on another occasion, Elder Holland observed, "Too many people . . . want to sin and call it psychology."[24] His two comments may appear to be contradictory but are in reality examples of the Prophet Joseph Smith's "contrarieties" mentioned earlier. Some experiences with depression are linked with deliberate and sometimes sinful behavior, and others are not.

Even though I do not fully understand how the Savior heals us from our physical, spiritual, and emotional afflictions, I do know that His atoning sacrifice makes these blessings possible. Having personally experienced the blessings of the healing power of Christ and having counseled with literally thousands of individuals and families who have also been strengthened and healed of their afflictions, I have witnessed what the prophet Enos described as having his concerns "swept away" (Enos 1:6) as he received the blessings of the Atonement of Jesus Christ.

For those of us who experience sorrow and depression in

part because of our own sins or the sins of others, President Boyd K. Packer taught: "Save for those few who defect to perdition after having known a fulness, there is no habit, no addiction, no rebellion, no transgression, no offense exempted from the promise of complete forgiveness." In the same conference address, President Packer described the process by which we are healed through the Atonement of Christ:

> When an offense is minor, so simple a thing as an apology will satisfy the law. Most mistakes can be settled between us and the Lord, and that should be done speedily (see D&C 109:21). It requires a confession to Him, and whatever obvious repairs need to be made. . . . To earn forgiveness, one must make restitution. That means you give back what you have taken or ease the pain of those you have injured. But sometimes you cannot give back what you have taken because you don't have it to give. If you have caused others to suffer unbearably . . . it is not within your power to give it back. There are times you cannot mend that which you have broken. Perhaps the offense was long ago, or the injured refused your penance. Perhaps the damage was so severe that you cannot fix it no matter how desperately you want to.

I believe President Packer's explanation can also be applied to many of the mental and emotional challenges we face. Just as there are some sins and mistakes for which it is impossible to make restitution, there are also some psychological disorders and emotional afflictions we experience that we are powerless to overcome on our own. President Packer concluded his remarkable statement by sharing an insight that is vital to helping us understand the purpose and power of the Atonement of Jesus Christ: "Restoring what you cannot restore, healing the wound you cannot heal, fixing that which you broke and you cannot fix is the very purpose of the atonement of Christ. When your desire is firm and you are willing to pay the 'uttermost farthing' (see Matt. 5:25–26), the law of restitution is suspended. Your obligation is transferred to the Lord. He will settle your accounts."[25]

Each one of us has spiritual, physical, and emotional weaknesses and afflictions that are beyond our ability to understand or to heal. There are also other problems we have in our personal lives, and in the lives of those we love, for which we do not have the solutions. These afflictions, in the words of Abinadi, can all be "swallowed up in Christ" (Mosiah 16:8) as we have faith in Him, repent of our sins, and keep sacred covenants. I believe the Savior can work miracles in our lives as He did in the life of the centurion's servant, when He promised, "I will come and heal him" (Matt. 8:7).

Job: "Darkness in the Daytime" (Job 5:14)

The biblical account of Job provides an important example of an individual whose emotional and physical burdens were multiplied by well-meaning friends who attempted to associate his suffering with his sins. By "blaming the victim," Job's friends may very well have contributed to an innocent victim becoming an angry accomplice. In the beginning of the scriptural account, Job endures the death of his children and his own physical afflictions and emotional burdens with a remarkable degree of humility and submission: "The Lord gave, and the Lord hath taken away; blessed be the name of the Lord. . . . Shall we receive good at the hand of God, and shall we not receive evil?" (Job 1:21; 2:10). But as Job's sufferings and sorrows continued over time, his resolve weakened, his faith faded, and he became both angry and depressed—especially when he engaged in conversations with his critics. Whether historical or allegorical (or both), the book of Job offers many lessons for those experiencing overwhelming physical, emotional, and spiritual pain. And perhaps there are equally important lessons for those who are attempting to assist those in need.

Blaming the Victim

Eliphaz, one of Job's friends, reminded Job of his former faithfulness and previous position of leadership in the community and then rebuked him by sermonizing that the Lord doesn't allow the righteous to suffer unless they have turned against God (see Job 4:3–7). Much of the book of Job is an account of the confrontations between Job and his friends concerning Job's alleged culpability in bringing about his own problems, including the deaths of his children. The judgments Eliphaz make against Job are an example of what King Benjamin warned against in the Book of Mormon when he stated: "Perhaps thou shalt say: The man has brought upon himself his misery; therefore I will stay my hand, and will not give unto him of my food, nor impart unto him of my substance that he may not suffer, for his punishments are just—But I say unto you, O man, whosoever doeth this the same hath great cause to repent; and except he repenteth of that which he hath done he perisheth forever, and hath no interest in the kingdom of God. For behold, are we not all beggars?" (Mosiah 4:17–19).

Eliphaz zealously expressed his judgments, wanting Job to understand and admit his sins, but like most criticisms, they were destructive. President James E. Faust (1920–2007) once counseled: "Your criticism may be worse than the conduct you are trying to correct."[26] Reverend Barbara Brown Taylor expressed that sometimes the most damaging criticisms of others we can make are those that include "religious" motives: "As a general rule," Reverend Taylor taught, "I would say that human beings never behave more badly toward one another than when they believe they are protecting God."[27]

Self-righteous judgments and criticisms made by others are some of the many burdens that Job bore in his day and that many individuals and families bear in our own day as they endure the stigma associated with mental illness. President Dieter F. Uchtdorf provided a profound, succinct, and emphatic answer to these concerns with his counsel: "Stop it!"

He went on to say, "It's that simple. We simply have to stop judging others and replace judgmental thoughts and feelings with a heart full of love for God and His children."[28]

The Great Test of Life

A careful reading of the book of Job provides ample evidence that Job wasn't one of the "evil doers" (Job 8:20) his self-righteous friends judged him to be, but we also learn that neither was he as "perfect and upright" (Job 1:1) as he is sometimes portrayed. Job's murmurings against God show that he was probably a lot like you and me if we were to lose most everything dear to us, including our family, and endure the physical, spiritual, and emotional suffering described in the scriptural record. The story of Job allows those who believe in God but who endure serious afflictions, including the unjust criticisms of others, to identify with someone who endured similar suffering.

Even though Job progressed slowly, and sometimes rebelliously, to fully submitting to the will of God, his witness of the Redeemer is a powerful reminder of his great faith in the face of inconceivable adversity. Job was angry and bitter and questioned God, but he never gave up. Even after an extended period of suffering that included the loss of seven sons and three daughters and his health, wealth, and position in the community, Job proclaimed: "For I know that my redeemer liveth, and that he shall stand at the latter day upon the earth: And though after my skin worms destroy this body, yet in my flesh shall I see God" (Job 19:25–26). President Henry B. Eyring taught: "The great test of life is to see whether we will hearken to and obey God's commands in the midst of the storms of life. It is not to endure storms, but to choose the right while they rage."[29] Job didn't endure his mortal afflictions perfectly, but there has been only One who has.

The scriptures and the history of the Church are replete with examples of good men and women who suffered mental and emotional problems that were not caused by faithlessness or disobedience. The book of Job also demonstrates the challenges and bitterness people experience when they judge, blame, and attempt to shame others—including God. Job's bitterness toward God, his friends, and anyone else who didn't see things his way were clearly expressions of the pain he was experiencing. This story illustrates the precept taught by President Boyd K. Packer that "often, very often, we are punished as much by our sins as we are for them."[30] Jane Clayson Johnson, a world-class journalist and a woman of faith who courageously confronted her own "dark night of the soul," quoted the following statement: "Depression is a ball and chain. Some people drag it. Other people swing it."[31] Job was one who swung his ball and chain with fury. Perhaps we can learn from his weaknesses and his strengths, as well as his failures and successes.

Accepting Personal Responsibility

While discussing the identity of the apostle who would, in the coming day, betray the Savior, "every one" of the ancient apostles asked Jesus, "Lord, is it I?" (Matt. 26:21–22). This question can be helpful as we attempt to determine the part we may play in the problems we face, but it is imperative to remember that blaming ourselves or blaming others (especially God) will only add to our problems. Clinical research suggests that blaming ourselves and blaming others (even when we or they are guilty)—are both related to a wide variety of mental health concerns.[32] Blaming and shaming ourselves or others isn't helpful. Accepting responsibility for our own sins and mistakes, and helping others to do the same (when we are authorized), is conducive to good mental health and emotional well-being.[33]

Expressing sincere praise and sharing constructive correction have also been found to strengthen relationships. Psychologists and researchers Drs. John and Julie Gottman report, "For every negative interaction during conflict, a stable and happy marriage [and family] has five (or more) positive interactions."[34] The ratio of five positive to one negative interaction has been reported to have a healing influence on individuals, marriages, families, and organizations alike.[35]

The following diagram illustrates the spectrum of the principles of correction and praise, ranging from the negative extreme of blame to another negative extreme, flattery (i.e., insincere praise intended to further one's own interests).

```
                CORRECTION       PRAISE
                     |              |
——————————————————————————————————————————————
                     |              |
BLAME                                          FLATTERY
```

Hannah

The Old Testament includes many accounts of those who struggled with emotional and spiritual pain, including the story of Hannah, the mother of the prophet Samuel. Before Hannah gave birth to Samuel, she suffered for many years because of her inability to conceive and bear children. Hannah was also burdened by the constant criticism of her husband's second wife, Peninnah. The scriptural account begins by describing the difficult events surrounding the yearly trip made by Hannah's husband, Elkanah, and his wives to the temple in Jerusalem to worship God by offering sacrifice:

> And this man went up out of his city yearly to worship and to sacrifice unto the Lord of hosts in Shiloh. . . . And when the time was that Elkanah offered [sacrifice at the temple], he gave to Peninnah his wife, and to all her sons and her daughters, portions [of the sacrifice]: But unto Hannah he gave a worthy portion; for he loved Hannah: but the Lord had shut up her womb. And her adversary [Peninnah] also provoked her sore, to make her fret, because the Lord had shut up her womb. And as he did so year by year, when she went up to the house of the Lord, so she provoked her; therefore she wept, and did not eat. (1 Sam. 1:3–7)

The Diagnostic and Statistical Manual, the guide used by mental health professionals to diagnose and treat mental illness, includes the following criteria for the diagnosis of depression: (1) "decrease or increase in appetite nearly every day" and (2) "depressed mood most of the day, nearly every day, as indicated by either subjective report (e.g., feels sad, empty, hopeless) or observation made by others (e.g., appears tearful)."[36] These symptoms usually last for several weeks at the very least.

Elkanah attempted to comfort Hannah by saying, "Why weepest thou? and why eatest thou not? and why is thy heart grieved? am not I better to thee than ten sons?" (1 Sam. 1:8). Though Hannah's response is not recorded, it is evident that her husband's attempt to comfort her by encouraging her to "count her blessings" was unsuccessful. She continued to seek relief through prayer: "And she was in bitterness of soul, and prayed unto the Lord, and wept sore. And she vowed a vow, and said, O Lord of hosts, if thou wilt indeed look on the affliction of thine handmaid, and remember me, and not forget thine handmaid, but wilt give unto thine handmaid a man child, then I will give him unto the Lord all the days of his life, and there shall no razor come upon his head" (1 Sam. 1:10–11).

Eli, the presiding priest at the temple, observed Hannah's grief-filled prayer and concluded that she had been drinking alcohol and that her thoughts and actions had become compromised: "And it came to pass, as she continued praying before the Lord, that Eli marked [i.e., observed] her mouth. Now Hannah, she spake in her heart; only her lips moved, but her voice was not heard: therefore Eli thought she had been drunken" (1 Sam. 1:12–13). The use of alcohol as a means of dealing with despair appears to have been a problem anciently as it is in the present, but alcohol wasn't among Hannah's problems. Her despair, while difficult to bear, motivated her to turn to the only legitimate source of healing she knew—God.

The next several verses include an informative and revealing conversation between Hannah and the high priest Eli: "And Eli said unto her, How long wilt thou be drunken? put away thy wine from thee. And Hannah answered and said, No, my lord, I am a woman of a sorrowful spirit: I have drunk neither wine nor strong drink, but have poured out my soul before the Lord. Count not thine handmaid for a daughter of Belial [wickedness or worthlessness]: for out of the abundance of my complaint and grief have I spoken hitherto" (1 Sam. 1:14–16). Eli then instructed and promised Hannah: "Go in peace: and the God of Israel grant thee thy petition that thou hast asked of him." Hannah responded in faith, "Let thine handmaid find grace in thy sight." We then learn that Hannah "went her way, and did eat, and her countenance was no more sad" (1 Sam. 1:17–18).

Hannah and Elkanah returned home, and in due time Hannah conceived and gave birth to a son—Samuel. Hannah was true to the vow she had made before Samuel was conceived, for at the appropriate time she took him to the temple and "lent him to the Lord" (1 Sam. 1:28). Hannah's maternal and symbolic sacrifice demonstrates that the vow she took during her depressed state represented her love for the Lord and was not simply a way of bargaining with God to fulfill her own desires. It was also remarkable, perhaps even miraculous, that Hannah's despair lifted before, not after, she was blessed with the child she wanted so desperately. It appears that Hannah's despair was "swept away" (Enos 1:6), at least in part, because of her faith in the promise given to her by the Lord through one of His authorized servants.

Hannah's story is an important example of someone who experienced feelings of despair but who was not guilty of grievous sin. Even if she did not suffer from a major depressive disorder, Hannah's experience with infertility was devastating and life altering. Hannah's story represents the feelings of many couples in our own day who suffer similar concerns. The following statement extracted from the pages of a research journal describes some of the sobering implications of infertility: "The impact of infertility can have deleterious social and psychological consequences on the individual, from overt ostracism or divorce to more subtle forms of social stigma leading to isolation and mental distress. In some cultures, motherhood is the only way for women to enhance status in their family and community. In the United States, specialists who study infertility have noted that infertile couples are one of the 'most neglected and silent minorities.'"[37]

Most parents experience genuine sadness and grief at the loss of a child, and children will grieve at the death of their parents, even if it is perceived as "their time to go." Life is painful, and each one us have experienced and will yet experience sadness related to a host of different kinds of losses—physical, emotional, and spiritual. President Boyd K. Packer once taught that sadness, disappointment, and failure are a necessary part of the human experience:

> We live in a day when the adversary stresses on every hand the philosophy of instant gratification. We seem to demand *instant* everything, including instant solutions to our problems. We are indoctrinated that somehow we should always be instantly emotionally comfortable. . . . It was meant to be that life would be a challenge. To suffer some anxiety, some depression, some disappointment, even some failure is normal. Teach our members that if they have a good, miserable day once in a while, or several in a row, to stand steady and face them. Things will straighten out. There is great purpose in our struggle in life.[38]

The stories of President George Albert Smith, Job, and Hannah are representative of good and faithful people across time and around the world who have loved and served God, loved their families and neighbors, and yet have done so while suffering from feelings of sorrow and despair. This chapter is only a brief introduction to their stories and many others like them whose stories are found in scripture, the history of Church, and in families and communities everywhere. See chapters 5 and 6 for discussions on how sorrow and depression can be addressed from both clinical and spiritual perspectives.

CHAPTER 2

ANXIETY AND THE GRACE OF JESUS CHRIST

". . . because of my over anxiety for you."
—*Jacob 4:18*

Anxiety is the most common mental health concern in the United States and throughout the world.[1] The National Institute of Mental Health recently reported that 19 percent of adults in America (forty million men and women) suffer with clinical symptoms of anxiety.[2] Similar to the different expressions of depression, the severity of anxiety ranges on a spectrum from the feelings of anxiousness we all experience to the anxiety that is debilitating. Examples of anxiousness, or "normal" anxiety, include the anticipation of stressful situations, such as speaking in public and meeting new people; concerns over health, family, or work issues; taking part in important meetings; participating in social gatherings; anticipating an important letter or phone call; and so on. Smells, sights, sounds, and emotions connected to past events can also trigger anxiety. The anxiety most people experience

- is generally related to a specific situation or concern.
- lasts as long as the problem or situation exists.
- has an intensity that is generally proportional to the problem.
- is a rational response to a realistic problem.

Most experiences we have with feelings of anxiety are not

evidence of mental illness. The following example, written by a psychiatrist who is also a mountain climber, illustrates how some anxiety can be intense and overwhelming but also normal:

> If an individual experienced a full-blown panic attack when, as a lead climber toward the top of a 1500-foot cliff, he loses his grip and falls 40 feet before his rope catches him and he hangs dangling looking a long way down the mountain side, no psychiatrist I know would consider this to be a psychopathological phenomenon. A panic attack is not—in and of itself—psychopathological. It only becomes pathology when it occurs in certain contexts—at times and in places when it should not.[3]

Both anxiety and fear can be normal and protective parts of the human experience. "*Fear* is the emotional response to real or perceived imminent threat, whereas, *anxiety* is anticipation of future threat."[4] The following diagram illustrates the contrasts between normal anxiety (anxiousness) and the anxiety or fear than can be debilitating. Also included is the contrast between "the *peace* of God, which passeth all understanding" (Philip. 4:7; emphasis added) and the attitude of *complacency*, which the prophet Nephi described as mistakenly believing "all is well in Zion" (2 Ne. 28:21).

	PEACE	ANXIOUSNESS	
COMPLACENCY			ANXIETY

Most feelings of anxiousness are associated with specific life events that are short-term and become manageable as life progresses. Some forms of anxiousness have also been demonstrated to "enhance motivation and achievement."[5] "If you're not nervous," the jazz musician Miles Davis once said, "you're not paying attention."[6] Counseling and psychotherapy can be very effective in treating debilitating anxiety.[7] Treating someone who is anxious with medication is generally not necessary but may be helpful when feelings of anxiety are excessive, consistent, difficult to control or stop, and begin to significantly interfere with everyday life.

More serious manifestations of anxiety include clinical diagnoses such as post-traumatic stress disorder (PTSD), obsessive-compulsive disorder (OCD), attention deficit hyperactivity disorder (ADHD), and agoraphobia (a disabling fear of places and circumstances). Medication and counseling (therapy) can be helpful in treating these clinical kinds of anxiety that dis-order life, impair health, complicate the lives of those afflicted, and make life more difficult for families, friends, and associates. Clinical anxiety

- is "free floating," meaning that it isn't generally related to a specific problem or event.
- has an intensity that is generally not proportional to the problem or concern.
- is unrealistic and includes supposed consequences that are unlikely.
- may last for weeks, months, and years—even after many of the identified "problems" have been resolved.
- may seem impossible to control or overcome.
- may contribute to the chronic avoidance of situations or people that the person with anxiety believes may trigger fear.[8]

Scrupulosity

Some of the most faithful and hardworking Latter-day Saints I know who suffer with anxiety are found among the young elders and sisters with whom I served as missionaries in West Africa. As their mission president, I too was anxious in my own way—anxious to assist them in working through their anxieties and finding joy in their service. One of these remarkable missionaries graciously granted permission for me to share key parts of his experiences with anxiety:

> Although not guilty of serious sin, the emotions I felt were what you expect to be associated with serious

transgression. I spoke with the MTC [Missionary Training Center] president, who reassured me that I was worthy to serve a mission. His reassurance only aided me for a day or so. Anxiety quickly returned. I prayed to be forgiven often and did all I could to find peace, but it was to no avail. I entered the mission field and found no peace. . . . I felt an emptiness; I more or less stopped trying to improve myself. This, however, was not a good solution. As I tried to improve, the anxiety came back and even worsened. At times I suffered so much that I could work no longer. I did not recognize that I was suffering from a mental illness, but instead I thought I was feeling guilt for sin. The only relief I could find was from confessing my mistakes to my mission president. At first, I was focused on mistakes and sins of a more sexual nature and as time went on, I confessed every sin of this nature that I could think of. I then began to unhealthily obsess on other sins and mistakes, such as speaking out of anger.[9]

This young man was suffering with a type of anxiety known as "scrupulosity," defined as "a psychological disorder primarily characterized by pathological guilt or obsession associated with moral or religious issues that is often accompanied by compulsive moral or religious observance and is highly distressing and maladaptive."[10] This young elder had experienced anxiety in the form of obsessive-compulsive behavior before his mission but never to the degree that it had become debilitating. Missionaries can often remain in the mission field and still address their emotional or physical concerns; other times it is best for them to return home and receive specialized psychological and medical treatment. This particular missionary returned home early, received additional help, and was able to return to the mission field. He had a very successful mission, but his service wasn't without difficulty.

This faithful young man described some of the solutions he discovered in dealing with what the Book of Mormon prophet Jacob described as "*over* anxiety" (Jacob 4:18; emphasis added): "My healing, while greatly attributed to counseling and medication, was only made possible by a deeper understanding of the grace of Jesus Christ. I had learned about grace earlier in my life but never really understood it. My first experience with understanding grace came during the beginning months of my mission when confessing to my mission president. He told me 'grace, by definition, is undeserved.' *I never before thought that I could gain something from God that I did not deserve.*"[11]

During one of our first interviews as missionary and mission president, I observed how similar this young man's anxieties were to those expressed by the Protestant reformer Martin Luther (1483–1546) when he first entered the monastery and began his training to become a Catholic priest. The story of the young Luther proved helpful to this missionary and provides an instructive example of an individual whose challenges with anxiety were turned to his good and to the good of all humankind. Luther's wrestle with anxiety was a major factor in bringing about the Protestant Reformation and in helping prepare the way for the later Restoration of the fullness of the gospel of Jesus Christ through the Prophet Joseph Smith. In many ways, Luther's story is our story and can help many of us better understand the "why" behind some of the problems we face and the beauty and power of the grace of Jesus Christ to heal those in need.

Martin Luther and Anxiety

From his personal writings we learn that young Martin Luther began his ministry as an exceptionally faithful and obedient Augustinian monk. After an initial year of peace, Luther began to experience feelings of guilt, anxiety, and despair. From Luther's own account we read:

> When I was a monk, I made a great effort to live according to the requirements of the monastic rule. I made a practice of confessing and reciting all my sins, but always with prior contrition; I went to confession frequently, and I performed the assigned penances faithfully. Nevertheless,

my conscience could never achieve certainty but was always in doubt and said: "You have not done this correctly. You were not contrite enough. You omitted this in your confession." Therefore, the longer I tried to heal my uncertain, weak, and troubled conscience with human traditions, the more uncertain, weak, and troubled I continually made it. In this way, by observing human traditions, I transgressed them even more; and by following the righteousness of the monastic order, I was never able to reach it.[12]

Luther's words provide a description that is familiar to many Latter-day Saints who attempt to overcome anxiety or depression by working harder at being more obedient, only to discover their problems become worse. Many of us seek to solve our emotional problems by praying more frequently and studying our scriptures with greater intensity. We attend the temple more often and serve in our callings more faithfully—all to prove to ourselves and to God that we are worthy of the blessings we are seeking. In many situations, exact obedience can lead to miracles, but in other circumstances, obsessive obedience becomes a manifestation of what the Book of Mormon prophet Jacob described as "looking beyond the mark" (Jacob 4:14). Mental health professionals and academics alike use the word *legalism* to describe this same overzealousness. President M. Russell Ballard addressed this doctrinal distortion as follows:

> No matter how hard we work, no matter how much we obey, no matter how many good things we do in this life, it would not be enough were it not for Jesus Christ and His loving grace. On our own we cannot earn the kingdom of God—no matter what we do. Unfortunately, there are some within the Church who have become so preoccupied with performing good works that they forget that those works—as good as they may be—are hollow unless they are accompanied by a complete dependence on Christ.[13]

As an Augustinian monk, Martin Luther was a part of a religious order within the Catholic Church named after St.

Augustine (AD 354–430). Augustinian monks had a reputation for strict moral and physical discipline. During Luther's time, those following the Augustinian order slept and studied in small and generally unheated rooms. In addition to making vows of chastity, obedience, and poverty, Luther and the other monks of his order engaged in formal worship beginning each day between and 1:00 and 2:00 a.m. These sessions normally lasted forty-five minutes each and were held seven times throughout the rest of the night and following day. The young Luther attempted to prove his devotion to God, and to himself, by getting up earlier and staying awake later. "I was a good monk," Luther described, "and kept the rule of my order so strictly that I may say that if ever a monk got to heaven by his monkery, it was I. All my brothers in the monastery who knew me will bear me out. If I had kept on any longer, I should have killed myself with vigils, prayers, reading, and other work."[14]

Though for most, increased obedience can be a necessary part of what President Russell M. Nelson has described as living in a "higher and holier way,"[15] for others such a response can be a distorted form of obedience that can lead to crippling anxiety and serious depression. Like Luther, there are Latter-day Saints who are anxiously working at being men and women of faith, only to find themselves emotionally drained, spiritually weak, and psychologically impaired. Many such individuals, in the past and the present, report feeling abandoned by God (see D&C 121:1; Ps. 13:1). For some, legalistic obedience (keeping the commandments to receive blessings) is the only kind of obedience they know; they haven't yet come to understand, nor have they experienced, the redemptive and enabling blessings of the grace of Jesus Christ.

For several years Luther amplified his efforts at becoming a more obedient monk, but his feelings of anxiety and doubt only increased. His writings reveal that other monks with whom he served experienced similar feelings: "I saw many who tried with great effort and the best of intentions to do everything possible to appease their conscience," he wrote. "They wore hair shirts; they fasted; they prayed; they tormented and wore out their bodies with various exercises so severely that if they had been made of iron, they would have been crushed. And yet the more they labored, the greater their terrors became."[16] Later in his life, Luther looked back on his troubled life as a young monk and identified the core of his confusion as follows: "I lost touch with Christ the Savior and Comforter and made of him the jailer and hangman of my poor soul."[17]

Church Attendance and Confession

Like many people of faith, Martin Luther looked to his religious beliefs and spiritual leaders to help him understand and overcome his feelings of anxiety and guilt. Specifically, he turned to the sacraments of his church, but he was not able to find the peace he was seeking. Commenting on his participation in confession to his church leaders and taking part in mass, Luther recorded: "After confession and the celebration of Mass I was never able to find rest in my heart."[18] Confession became an unfruitful ordeal for both Luther and those to whom he "confessed frequently, often daily, and for as long as six hours on a single occasion."[19]

In my service as a priesthood leader, I have never worked with Church members who wanted to confess their sins for six hours at a time, but several individuals (including the young missionary described earlier) requested daily contact, wanting to confess their sins and seeking reassurance. Confessing sins and receiving counsel from leaders with priesthood keys who represent the Lord and His church are a necessary part of forgiveness for serious sins, but confession that is compulsive, and sometimes even contrived, can also be evidence of anxiety that needs to be recognized and addressed by priesthood leaders and perhaps mental health professionals.

Fasting

Prophets (see Isa. 58:6) and scholars agree that fasting (going without food and drink for a period of time) can be very helpful in facing physical, spiritual, and psychological crises.[20] Fasting for the wrong reasons, however, can become a part of a larger problem. Luther recorded: "I almost fasted myself to death, for again and again I went for three days without taking a drop of water or a morsel of food."[21] While he acknowledged that fasting had a legitimate place in Christian worship, Luther warned that those who practiced fasting beyond its intended purpose (as he had) would "simply ruin their health and drive themselves mad."[22]

Prayer

Luther's scrupulous devotion to prayer, a central part of a monk's daily routine, also appears to have added to his burden. Luther stated: "I chose twenty-one saints and prayed to three every day when I celebrated mass; thus I completed the number every week. I prayed especially to the Blessed Virgin, who with her womanly heart would compassionately appease her Son."[23] Luther reported that instead of bringing the relief he sought, his extra devotion to fasting and prayer "made [his] head split."[24] While no mortal can accurately judge the origin of Luther's guilt, anxiety, and despair, it is clear that he was desperate to understand and to resolve his constant concerns.

Perfectionism

In his general conference address entitled "Be Ye Therefore Perfect—Eventually," Elder Jeffrey R. Holland addressed some of the same issues Martin Luther faced with what is commonly described as "perfectionism": "Around the Church I hear many who struggle with this issue: 'I am just not good enough.' 'I fall so far short.' 'I will never measure up.' I hear this from teenagers. I hear it from missionaries. I hear it from new converts. I hear it from lifelong members. One insightful Latter-day Saint, Sister Darla Isackson, has observed that Satan has somehow managed to make covenants and commandments seem like curses and condemnations. For some he has turned the ideals and inspiration of the gospel into self-loathing and misery-making."

Elder Holland continued, "With a willingness to repent and a desire for increased righteousness always in our hearts, I would hope we could pursue personal improvement in a way that doesn't include getting ulcers or anorexia, feeling depressed or demolishing our self-esteem." He then provided the following counsel, quoting the ancient prophet Moroni:

> "Yea, come unto Christ, and be perfected in him . . . ," Moroni pleads. "Love God with all your might, mind and strength, then . . . *by his grace ye may be perfect in Christ*" [Moro. 10:32]. Our only hope for true perfection is in receiving it as a gift from heaven—we can't "earn" it. Thus, the grace of Christ offers us not only salvation from sorrow and sin and death but also salvation from our own persistent self-criticism.[25]

While the teachings of latter-day prophets and those espoused by Protestant reformers differ in some ways, there are also profound similarities with respect to the blessings of the grace of Jesus Christ.

The Grace of Jesus Christ

Luther's journey toward healing gained momentum when he accepted an invitation by his leaders to pursue a doctoral degree and lecture on the Bible at Wittenberg University. Luther was surprised by the invitation but accepted the new assignment and began a serious study of the Bible, beginning with the book of Psalms, followed by the New Testament epistles, Romans, and Galatians. As he faithfully studied and taught the scriptures to his students and to the members of the various congregations for whom he had pastoral responsibility, Luther began to find answers to his spiritual and emotional concerns.[26] The insights he received and taught not only eased the burdens he bore and blessed the lives of the students and parishioners he taught, but they also changed the course of history and provided an important example for each of us to follow.

While Luther considered several different scriptural texts vital to his and others' spiritual and psychological rebirth, the text he considered key to his personal transformation is found in the Apostle Paul's epistle to the Romans: "For therein is the righteousness of God revealed from faith to faith: as it is written, The just shall live by faith" (Rom. 1:17). In the beginning, Luther struggled to understand the scriptural phrase "the righteousness of God." Initially these words angered him to the point that he "hated the righteous God who punishes sinners."[27] But his gradual understanding of "God's righteousness" ultimately provided him the understanding and strength he was seeking: "But when by God's grace I pondered . . . 'the righteousness of God,' . . . I soon came to the conclusion that if we, as righteous men, ought to live from faith and if the righteousness of God contribute to the salvation of all who believe, then salvation won't be our merit but God's mercy. My spirit was thereby cheered. For it's by the righteousness of God that we're justified and saved through Christ."[28]

Luther came to understand that the "righteousness of God" wasn't a description of God's superior status and His anger toward the sinner, but rather it was a description of God's goodness and love for His children. The righteousness of God also reflects the truth that He will forgive us of our sins and provide strength to all who exercise faith in Christ, the truths He taught, and the sacrifice He made for each of us (see Rom. 4:25).

Another doctrinal truth Luther initially failed to understand was that personal peace and eternal salvation are not simply rewards for doing good works but are gifts made available through the Atonement of Jesus Christ. Some of these very same doctrinal misunderstandings and anxieties exist among Latter-day Saints today. Elder Dieter F. Uchtdorf explained: "Salvation cannot be bought with the currency of obedience; it is purchased by the blood of the Son of God. . . . *Our obedience to God's commandments comes as a natural outgrowth of our endless love and gratitude for the goodness of God.* This form of genuine love and gratitude will miraculously merge our works with God's grace."[29]

The Apostle Paul taught: "Knowing that a man is not justified by the works of the law, but by the faith of Jesus Christ, even we have believed in Jesus Christ, that we might be justified by the faith of Christ, and not by the works of the law" (Gal. 2:16).

All of Luther's prayers, fasting, confessions, and indulgences could never earn God's favor and bring Luther the blessings of peace and redemption he sought. Luther's compulsive praying, obsessive fasting, and initial study of the scriptures do not appear to have been motivated by a pharisaical desire to elicit the praise of his fellowmen but by his desire to be accepted by God, free from guilt, and liberated from a consuming fear of damnation. He simply didn't understand the graciousness and goodness of a loving God.

Luther's new understanding of the grace of Jesus Christ allowed him to truly have faith in Christ, accept God's forgiveness, have confidence in himself, and focus on the needs of others. After many years of anxiety and despair, he experienced peace in the conviction that the righteousness of the Redeemer had become his own.

The young missionary whom I described earlier, and many other elders and sisters much like him, reported similar experiences as they came to understand the grace of Christ.[30] The redemptive and enabling power of the grace of Christ allows us to be forgiven of our sins, transform our weakness into strength, and receive the peace we cannot obtain through our own righteousness, no matter how faithful and obedient we are. The prophet Lehi taught his son Jacob these same life-giving truths: "And behold, in thy childhood thou hast suffered afflictions and much sorrow, because of the rudeness of thy brethren. Nevertheless, Jacob, my firstborn in the wilderness, thou knowest the greatness of God; and he shall consecrate thine afflictions for thy gain. . . . Wherefore, I know that *thou art redeemed, because of the righteousness of thy Redeemer*; for thou hast beheld that in the fulness of time he cometh to bring salvation unto men (2 Ne. 2:1–3; emphasis added).

Cheap Grace

While some individuals take the "increased obedience" path to overcoming their imperfections (including mental and emotional issues), others embrace the opposite view and expect God to heal them without expending their own best efforts. Taking the doctrine of grace beyond what the Savior and His servants have taught cheapens and changes this most important doctrine into a distortion that mocks the very purpose of the Atonement of Jesus Christ. German pastor and theologian Dietrich Bonhoeffer (1906–1945) warned against accepting what he described as "cheap grace":

> Cheap grace is the preaching of forgiveness without requiring repentance, baptism without church discipline, Communion without confession, absolution without personal confession. Cheap grace is grace without discipleship, grace without the cross, grace without Jesus Christ. . . . [True] grace is *costly* because it calls us to follow, and it is *grace* because it calls us to follow *Jesus Christ*. It is costly because it costs a man his life, and it is grace because it gives a man the only true life. It is costly because it condemns sin, and grace because it justifies the sinner. Above all, it is *costly* because it cost God the life of his Son.[31]

The Book of Mormon anti-Christ Nehor taught a similar false doctrine: "All mankind should be saved at the last day, and that they need not fear nor tremble, but that they might lift up their heads and rejoice; for the Lord had created all men, and had also redeemed all men; and, in the end, all men should have eternal life" (Alma 1:4).

Another Book of Mormon anti-Christ, Korihor, taught the

opposite and equally false doctrine that "every man fared in this life according to the management of the creature; therefore every man prospered according to his genius, and that *every man conquered according to his strength*; and whatsoever a man did was no crime" (Alma 30:17; emphasis added). Korihor provided another deceptive doctrinal example of legalism—the idea that we can save ourselves through our own good works. The following diagram illustrates the contrasts between the grace of God, the works of humankind, and the counterfeit doctrines of cheap grace and legalism.

	GRACE	WORKS	
CHEAP GRACE			LEGALISM

Professor Robert Millet provided an insightful summary of the relationship between the grace of Christ and our own good works: "God and man are at work together in the salvation of the human soul. The real question is not whether we are saved by grace or by works. The real questions are these: In whom do I trust? On whom do I rely?"[32]

Research on Grace and Mental Health

In 2017, two of my colleagues and I designed the first formal research study ever published on the relationships among the grace of Christ, legalism, and the mental health of members of The Church of Jesus Christ of Latter-day Saints. The data for our study, collected from 635 Latter-day Saints, are consistent with the experiences of Martin Luther and the missionary whose story I shared earlier. Our research clearly indicates that understanding and experiencing the grace of God has a positive influence on mental health.

We also learned that an individual's legalistic beliefs (i.e., we can work our way to happiness and to heaven) are associated with decreased mental health because these beliefs interfere with an individual's ability to experience the grace of Christ.[33] Our research also supports President Ballard's comment that some Latter-day Saints become "so preoccupied with performing good works" that they forget the importance of having a "complete dependence on Christ."[34] The following graph illustrates how individuals in our study who

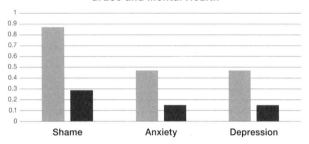

Grace and Mental Health

understood, experienced, and embraced the grace of Christ (dark-gray bars) experienced shame, anxiety, and depression in comparison to those who believed God's love to be conditional on their obedience (light-gray bars).

Manifestations of Anxiety

The Diagnostic and Statistical Manual of Mental Disorders (DSM-5)[35] lists seven different anxiety disorders. The following descriptions are simplified introductions to these conditions. Please don't make the mistake of using these descriptions as diagnostic criteria for yourself or others but simply as a means of understanding the different kinds of anxiety individuals and families face.

- *Separation anxiety disorder*: Excessive fear or distress concerning separation from those to whom the individual has become closely attached.
- *Selective mutism*: Consistent inability to speak in some social settings or to some people even though they may do so in other situations. (Not speaking when learning a foreign language would not generally qualify.)

- *Specific phobia*: An irrational fear of specific objects or situations: animals, germs, insects, heights, flying, driving, medical procedures, seeing blood, etc.
- *Social anxiety disorder*: Fear or anxiety about social situations where the individual has heightened concern about being judged by others.
- *Panic disorder*: Recurrent panic attacks that come without warning. This disorder includes the anxiety people experience in anticipation over when the next incident will occur. Panic episodes often include such symptoms as accelerated heart rate, sweating, trembling, nausea, fear of dying, and feelings of "going crazy."
- *Agoraphobia*: Avoidance of situations or places that may produce increased anxiety such as use of public transportation or being in enclosed or open spaces.
- *Generalized anxiety disorder (GAD)*: Excessive anxiety, even though no "triggers" are apparent. The anxiety is of such magnitude that the individual's ability to function in day-to-day activities is seriously impaired. Fatigue, insomnia, headaches, shortness of breath, irritability, and hot flashes are common.[36]

While many people can identify with various parts of these different manifestations of anxiety, receiving a formal diagnosis of an anxiety disorder requires an evaluation by a mental health professional. The formal diagnosis would also include evidence of the symptoms being manifest over a specific period of time and of sufficient magnitude to seriously impede a person's ability to live the life they would like to live.

Examples of Those Who Have Suffered with Anxiety

By the time the poet Emily Dickinson (1830–1886) was forty years old, she refused to leave her home and often hid in her bedroom when longtime friends came to visit. She appears to have been afflicted with agoraphobia.[37] Other prominent people afflicted with agoraphobic anxiety include Charles Darwin (1809–1882)[38] and actress Kim Basinger.[39]

Some readers may be surprised to learn that Steve Young, Brigham Young University's all-American quarterback, who went on to become the Super Bowl MVP while playing for the San Francisco Forty-Niners, suffered with separation anxiety disorder. His symptoms first appeared when he was a child and lasted well into his professional career in the National Football League. Anxiety—not his professional career in the NFL—was also the reason Brother Young reports that he did not serve as a full-time missionary. From Steve's own words: "People thought my status as a football player had influenced my decision not to serve a mission, unaware that I was an eighth-string nobody [at BYU] when I made that decision. It was only the fear and anxiety that had held me back."[40] Brother Young explained some of what he eventually learned about his condition from the psychiatrist who initially treated him as an adult:

> He [the psychiatrist] told me there was a clinical name for my symptoms: separation anxiety disorder. I had never heard this term, and I wanted to know more. He said it usually manifests itself in children when they go off to kindergarten. After five years of being nurtured, fed, and cared for exclusively by parents, some children demonstrate great anxiety when they are first put into a classroom with twenty other children and a teacher who especially functions as a new parent. "Some kids cry all day," he explained. It's a lot of separation anxiety. Separation anxiety was what I had as a child. Anticipatory anxiety was what I had now.[41]

During a recent interview with Brother Young, he shared with me that one of the first nights in his life he spent away from his parents was his first night as a freshman at BYU. I asked Steve if given the choice of living his life over again without anxiety, would he choose to do so. His answer was revealing: "My first answer is 'yes,' it would be awesome to go through life and just experience [it] the way everyone else did. That would be so great because I could see everyone else really enjoying the things I just couldn't. But then here I am, and the richness that I feel, the strength, the depth that I feel. It would be different. And so in that way, I probably would get back in line for it again."

Steve believes his experiences with anxiety have helped him become the man he is today. I found Steve Young to be a man of intellectual depth and spiritual sensitivity—born, in part, from his wrestle with anxiety. He has shown great courage in facing anxiety, and a great deal of wisdom in seeking help from his parents, family, friends, colleagues, inspired Church leaders, and mental health professionals and, above all else, "being tethered to heaven."[42]

While I present treatment options for anxiety from both spiritual and psychological perspectives in chapters 5 and 6, we should remember that life, by divine design, is intended to be difficult. Anxiety, at least in its milder forms, is one of the "thorn[s] in the flesh" (2 Cor. 12:7) we all experience and, in the end, can be a part of the mortal experience that helps us understand our need for others, including our need for and dependence on God.

CHAPTER 3

PSYCHOTIC DISORDERS, SELF-DECEPTION, AND PERSONAL REVELATION

> "I had seen a vision;
> I knew it, and I knew that God knew it,
> and I could not deny it."
> —*Joseph Smith—History 1:25*

One of the first scholarly studies published on the relationship between religion and mental health focused on the personality, prophetic practices, and religious experiences of the Prophet Joseph Smith. In 1903, Isaac Woodbridge Riley (1869–1933), a recent graduate of Yale University, published his doctoral dissertation, entitled "The Founder of Mormonism: A Psychological Study of Joseph Smith, Jr." Riley's study of Joseph Smith and the Prophet's accounts of seeing and communicating with the Father and the Son and of the appearances of Moroni and other angelic messengers (see JS—H 1:17; D&C 128:20–21) led Riley to conclude that the Prophet's visions were the effects of "ophthalmic migraine[s]," coupled with epilepsy and melancholic depression.[1]

Riley's conclusions are representative of some clinicians and scholars in our day who believe religious belief and practice are "in many respects equivalent to irrational thinking and emotional disturbance. . . . The less religious [people] are, the more emotionally healthy they will be."[2] In comparison to the people they serve, psychiatrists, psychologists, and other mental health professionals are "more than twice as likely to claim no religion, three times more likely to describe religion as unimportant in their lives, and five times more likely to deny belief in God."[3] There are, however, many mental health professionals who are men and women of deep religious faith.

Though some individuals do suffer from psychotic disorders, faithful members of The Church of Jesus Christ of Latter-day Saints join many other people of faith in believing God has spoken and continues to communicate with His prophets and all who "hath ears to hear" (Matt. 13:9) in wonderful ways unrelated to mental illness. Latter-day Saints join much of the religious world in believing in the divine call of the prophet Abraham, that he "talked with the Lord, face to face, as one man talketh with another" (Abr. 3:11), and that the Lord also "spake unto Moses face to face, as a man speaketh unto his friend" (Ex. 33:11). The Lord taught how He communicates with His prophets when He stated: "If there be a prophet among you, I the Lord will make myself known unto him in a vision, and will speak unto him in a dream" (Num. 12:6).

In addition to revealing "his secret[s] unto his servants the prophets" (Amos 3:7) through visions and dreams, God also communicates with His sons and daughters in a variety of other ways, including personal prayer. A study conducted in 2008 reported that "as many as 97% of Americans pray, and 57% indicate that they pray one or more times each day."[4] A more recent comparison of different religious traditions revealed that the frequency of prayer increased between 2007 and 2014 for Christians (including Latter-day Saints) and Jews but declined for those who identify as Muslim, Hindu, or Buddhist. Combined, the percentage of those of all faiths who reported that they pray daily declined from 58 percent in 2007 to 55 percent in 2014. However, members of The Church of Jesus Christ of Latter-day Saints who reported praying daily increased from 82 percent to 85 percent during the same seven-year period.[5]

My three years as a mission president in Ghana, West Africa, reminded me that not only does God communicate with His children through prayer but He also provides counsel and comfort through visions and dreams. I was skeptical of the African people's revelatory experiences during my first few months of living and working among them, but when I began to see the fulfillment of their visions and dreams in my own life as well as in the lives of my missionaries and the people whom the missionaries were teaching, my doubts were transformed into a reverent awe of God's prophetic presence in the lives of the African people. The African Saints are inspiring examples of those whom Moses was describing when he stated, "Would God that all the Lord's people were prophets, and that the Lord would put his spirit upon them!" (Num. 11:29).

I join faithful Latter-day Saints around the world in believing that Adam, Abraham, Moses, and other prophets described in scripture, as well as the Prophet Joseph Smith and those who have succeeded him, are prophets of God and that Jesus Christ is the Son of God. We believe that the revelatory manifestations prophets have had and will yet experience come from God and are not psychotic delusions or inspired fictions. Latter-day Saints also believe that God speaks to all His children in very personal ways, though many don't recognize the divine origin of the wisdom and grace they receive.

We must, however, also acknowledge the reality of counterfeit revelations; the Prophet Joseph taught: "nothing is a greater injury to the children of men than to be under the influence of a false spirit when they think they have the Spirit of God."[6] Some of the "spiritual manifestations" people report are not from God or the adversary but are best understood as psychotic delusions. In a study conducted in Eastern Europe in 2008, 60 percent of the 295 individuals diagnosed with schizophrenia reported receiving visions, dreams, and revelations.[7]

During my career as a clinician and professor, and particularly in my service as a Church leader, I have met with Latter-day Saints who believed they had been commanded by God to rescue the membership (especially the leadership) of The Church of Jesus Christ of Latter-day Saints from apostasy. On

PSYCHOTIC DISORDERS, SELF-DECEPTION

one occasion, a man visiting my home ward stood in fast and testimony meeting and declared that he was Captain Moroni and that he had been sent by the Lord to call the ward to repentance. On two separate occasions, individuals shared with me what they believed to be their divine calls as translators of ancient scripture and gave me copies of what they believed to be inspired translations of the sealed portion of the Book of Mormon. I also once worked with a woman who believed that the father of the baby she was carrying was John the Revelator. Each of these individuals was sincere in their beliefs but was clearly experiencing a form of psychosis.

Psychotic delusions often include distorted expressions of the parts of people's lives that are most important to them. For those whose afflictions I have just described, their delusions were expressions of their religious beliefs. For others, such expressions might include their love for sports, art, science fiction, politics, or some other personal passion. I once met a man during my training at the Utah State Mental Hospital who adamantly believed he was the legendary baseball player Babe Ruth. When I got to know a little more about this very interesting man, I wasn't surprised to learn of his lifelong love for baseball. His mental illness was being expressed through a part of his life he loved.

It is a serious mistake, and even a breach of the covenants we have made with God, to label individuals who are suffering with mental illness as "mad" (1 Sam. 21:14), "nuts, "crazy," or "a quart low" or to mock them and the stories they believe to be true. In each of the incidences I have just mentioned (and a host of others), the individuals with whom I worked were wonderful people who, for one reason or another, had lost touch with reality and sincerely believed their own distorted realities. Those who suffer with these delusions have varying degrees of awareness concerning the validity of their experiences and varying degrees of agency and ability to trust or to distrust what they are experiencing. Some individuals are able to see their delusions for what they really are and, over time, are able to deal with them appropriately. Others completely believe their own stories and resent or are confused by any attempt to convince them otherwise.

One of the most important lessons I have learned over the years working with individuals who are suffering with emotional and psychological concerns is to interpret their various symptoms and diagnoses as being *descriptive*, but not *definitive*. In other words, even though someone might manifest the clinical symptoms of schizophrenia, depression, or some other mental disorder, I deliberately avoid thinking or speaking of these individuals as a "schizophrenic" or "bipolar," etc. While such definitive diagnostic descriptions can be helpful in developing a treatment plan and are often required for health insurance purposes, choosing not to label these individuals helps me remember their divine identities as sons and daughters of Heavenly Parents. Seeing others in this way also helps me appreciate the sacred responsibility I have as their brother to help them fulfill their mortal mission and one day return to their heavenly home—to eventually be whole and free of their mortal afflictions. The Prophet Joseph Smith once taught, "All the minds and spirits that God ever sent into the world are susceptible of enlargement."[8]

Like depression and anxiety, psychotic delusions can also be understood as existing on a continuum from slight to severe. A clinical diagnosis of a psychotic disorder, which very few people receive, is at one end of the continuum, and self-deception, a phenomenon we have all experienced, is at a separate but related position on the other end.

Self-Deception and Agency

Though most do not experience a psychotic disorder, each of us has had the common experience of believing something about ourselves or others that is not true. In the Book of Mormon, Amulek recorded his own experience with self-deception. After describing himself as a "man of no small reputation" and declaring he had "acquired much riches by the hand of [his] industry," Amulek states, "I never have known much of the ways of the Lord, and his mysteries and marvelous power." To his credit, he then corrects himself: "I said I never had known much of these things; but behold, I mistake, for I have seen much of his mysteries and his marvelous power; yea, even in the preservation of the lives of this people" (Alma 10:4–5).

Amulek then describes his self-deception in more detail: "Nevertheless, I did harden my heart, for I was called many times and I would not hear; therefore *I knew concerning these things, yet I would not know*; therefore I went on rebelling against God, in the wickedness of my heart" (Alma 10:6; emphasis added). The Apostle John described the act of self-deception as follows: "if we say that we have no sin, *we deceive ourselves*, and the truth is not in us" (1 John 1:8; emphasis added).

C. Terry Warner, an emeritus professor of philosophy at Brigham Young University, shared an important story, told by a man identified as "Marty," that can help each of us understand just how common it is to ignore personal inspiration and to engage in self-deception. The story also illustrates how deceiving ourselves can contribute to some of the emotional problems that can consume our lives: "The other night [at] about 2:00 a.m. I awoke to hear the baby crying. At that moment I had a fleeting feeling, a feeling that if I got up quickly, I might be able to see what was wrong before Carolyn would be awakened. It was a feeling that this was something I really ought to do. But I didn't get up to check on the baby."

The "fleeting feeling" Marty experienced to get up and see what was wrong with his baby and to selflessly serve his wife can be described in many ways, including "a prompting of conscience," "a moral imperative," "the light of Christ," "the Spirit of the Lord," "the Holy Ghost," and "a natural law," to name only a few. The Apostle Paul, writing about the Gentiles of his day, described this moral sense as "the law written in their hearts" (Rom. 2:15). Whatever we choose to call this unique knowledge, Marty didn't respond in a way that was consistent with what he sensed was the right thing to do:

> It bugged me that Carolyn wasn't waking up. I kept thinking it was her job to take care of the baby. She has her work and I have mine, and mine is hard. It starts early in the morning. She can sleep in. On top of that, I never know how to handle the baby anyway.
>
> I wondered if Carolyn was lying there waiting for me to get up. Why did I have to feel so guilty that I couldn't sleep? The only thing I wanted was to get to work fresh enough to do a good job. What was so selfish about that?[9]

Marty's self-deception included the narrative that he was the victim, his wife was the villain, and his thoughts, feelings, actions, and inactions were justified. In addition to his logical arguments, accusations, and self-excusing emotions, his physical fatigue was an integral part of his self-justification for not responding to his prompting. If he had been awakened by an alarm reminding him to get up and go skiing, his feelings would have been very different.

The thoughts, feelings, and physiological state Marty experienced all became a part of his self-deception. It would have been so much easier on everyone (including Marty) if he would have quickly responded to his original impression to awake, arise, and respond to the needs of his wife and child. A growing body of research indicates that we as individuals and the various cultures of which we are a part can contribute to the emotional problems and the relationship crises we experience, particularly as we engage in self-deception.[10]

Clarissa

A dear friend recently shared with me how she came to understand the relationship between her own moral agency and her experiences with depression and anxiety. Clarissa's way of understanding her experiences challenges the biological model of mental illness. In the first ten years of their marriage, Clarissa and her husband were "blessed with two daughters and five sons." Clarissa described her children as "my joy, the fulfillment of my girlhood dreams about motherhood." Between giving birth to children numbers five and six, Clarissa had a miscarriage, which was followed by "days and weeks [that] . . . were difficult and dark, full of self-doubt and deep sadness." Clarissa continued: "What started as a perhaps understandable response to difficulty and loss turned into nearly two and a half years of struggling with waves of anxiety, depression, and thoughts of suicide. I often couldn't eat and lost weight rapidly. Over time, I developed stomach ulcers. . . . I was often barely functioning. Everything looked impossible."

After eventually giving birth to her seventh child, Clarissa and her husband agreed that their family was complete. However, instead of being relieved, the reality of not being able to have more children was heartbreaking for Clarissa, and she began to experience serious psychological distress. She continued to "spiral downward," and in the midst of expressing anger toward God, Clarissa described His response: "[I] demanded of God that He let me go, let me die or break or escape somehow. When I heard the words, softly, 'Get up,' I was incredibly angry. Was He even hearing me?! My point was that I had gotten up and gotten up, and I wasn't getting up anymore. 'It's alright,' came the voice again. 'Get up.'"

At other times during this same period, Clarissa had additional promptings such as "pick up that sock . . . put it in the hamper" and "a further string of tiny promptings that lasted until [she] was moving again on [her] own." During a difficult conversation with her husband that focused on her needs, she felt the prompting, "He really needs you now." Clarissa reported, "I was sure I was the one who needed, but the prompting suggested otherwise." Clarissa concluded her story as follows:

> It took a long time for me to connect the dots, but I realized, as I began to heal, that one way of thinking about those years of depression is as a tutorial in agency. What the Spirit was teaching me, line upon line upon line upon

line, was that depression and anxiety weren't happening to me; they were something I was doing. And if I would listen, the Spirit would teach me to do something else, something truer, more sustainable, and most of all, more joyful.

One way I was doing depression and anxiety was by clinging to misperceptions about important things. I didn't know they were misperceptions, and I didn't realize that they were shaping (I would now say mis-shaping) my responses to everything. And I understood least of all that I was clinging to them. They were so natural to me that they seemed like the only way. Day after day, life was chipping away at my wrong-headedness and wrong-heartedness, showing me that if I went on seeing the world the way I did, nothing worked. I ended up suicidal, feeling that life and my own existence were simply not sustainable.

The saving grace was that, when I was willing to see it, the Spirit was always there, offering a better way. In that way the solution is simple, but not obvious, not easy, and not quick. Giving up the beliefs and feelings of one's whole life so far is a daunting process, and perhaps I just haven't been particularly cooperative, but in my experience it can take a long time. It would be years before I could begin to give a truer account of events, seeing God's hand where, at the time, I had thought Him absent or uncaring, and even more importantly, seeing my part in creating the mental anguish I had experienced as inevitable. Only when I learned to tell the story with my agency at the heart of it did I begin to see how I could respond to life and the people around me in happier and more loving ways.[11]

Clarissa's account illustrates the blessings that can be experienced when one has "a broken heart and a contrite spirit" (3 Ne. 9:20), even when the individual has every reason not to be patient, submissive, and teachable. Over a period of years, Clarissa came to understand her feelings of depression and anxiety for what they really were (at least for her) and found the peace she was seeking. I can honestly describe Clarissa as one of the most intellectually capable, emotionally aware, and spiritually sensitive people I know.

As illustrated in the stories of Clarissa and Marty, some of the emotional and psychological afflictions with which each of us suffer can be linked to the use and misuse of our own moral agency. Other afflictions, like some forms of depression, anxiety, and most of what we describe as schizophrenia and other psychotic disorders occur from no fault or failing of our own but are the consequences of living as mortal beings in a fallen world.

Schizophrenia and Other Psychotic Disorders

The "Schizophrenic Spectrum and Other Psychotic Disorders" section of *The Diagnostic and Statistical Manual of Mental Disorders* (DSM-5) includes seventeen separate but related diagnoses tied to psychotic disturbances. Since this chapter is intended to be a brief introduction, I won't describe these disorders in detail, but detailed descriptions can be found in Marleen Williams, Dean Belnap, and John Livingstone's *Matters of the Mind: Latter-day Saint Helps for Mental Health* (Salt Lake City: Deseret Book, 2008), 196–219.

Though schizophrenia affects less than 1 percent of people worldwide, it is considered one of the most severe of all psychiatric disorders and requires considerable time of family, friends, Church leaders, and others who care for an individual suffering with this complicated disorder. Schizophrenia afflicts men and women in equal numbers. Because the word *schizophrenia* means "split mind," the condition is often confused with multiple personality disorder, which was made famous by movies such as *American Psycho*, *The Three Faces of Eve*, and *Sybil*. Multiple personality disorder is now referred to as dissociative identity disorder and shouldn't be confused with schizophrenia. Schizophrenia has been defined as follows: "A mental illness that is characterized by disturbances in thought (such as delusions), perception (such as hallucinations), and behavior (such as disorganized speech or catatonic behavior), by a loss of emotional responsiveness and extreme apathy, and by noticeable deterioration in the level of functioning in everyday life."[12]

Even though neither cause nor cure for schizophrenia (and related disorders) have been identified in the scientific literature, advances in research and treatment have made it possible for many of those who suffer from these disorders to live meaningful and rewarding lives. Psychiatrist Thomas McGlashan stated, "The certainty of negative prognosis in schizophrenia is a myth."[13] Many individuals diagnosed with schizophrenia live happy, meaningful, and productive lives.

Ben

Ben Paramore (not his real name) first began to suffer the symptoms of what would later be diagnosed as "schizoaffective disorder" when he was in his late teens. Even as Ben began to hear voices with greater regularity, he kept what he was experiencing to himself. He told himself that the voices would go away if he was able to "get more sleep," "take better care of himself," and "be more faithful," but the frequency and intensity of the symptoms continued to increase. He worried that if he shared what was happening to him, his family and friends would think he was "crazy" and he wouldn't be able to go on a mission, marry in the temple, or have a family. Ben recently shared with me the following description of his early experiences with what he later learned were the symptoms of schizophrenia:

> When I started my descent into mental illness as a teenager, my denial and delay of seeking help was primarily motivated by a fear. . . . If I truly was mentally ill, all my dreams were over. Some of it was stigma. I thought I'd be in a cell and in a white jacket for the rest of my life. . . . Even if I wasn't locked up, it would be impossible for me to do the things I wanted to do—having a family, going to school, having a job, having any sort of respect. Those things were not in the cards for someone with mental illness. Those fears kept me from treatment [and] were emotionally paralyzing.[14]

PSYCHOTIC DISORDERS, SELF-DECEPTION

Ben deliberately decided not to share his mental health problems with his family, bishop, stake president, or physician during the time he was preparing to serve a mission. He was called to serve in a foreign country and did so for nearly a year until the "voices" he was hearing "inside his head" began to be overwhelming. These symptoms became so oppressive that he decided to share his burden with the only person he believed would understand—Lydia. Lydia was a young woman whom Ben had met while attending Brigham Young University the year before he left on his mission, and he regularly exchanged letters with her during his mission. Even though Elder Paramore trusted Lydia not to tell anyone, she wisely chose to disclose what he had shared with her to her parents. Lydia's parents were able to ensure that the information about Elder Paramore's condition was quickly communicated to his mission president. In just a matter of hours, Elder Paramore was on a bus to the mission home and then on an airplane home to be diagnosed and treated for schizoaffective disorder.

Even though Elder Paramore initially felt betrayed by Lydia, he quickly came to realize that by sharing his "secret," she had helped save his life. Ben was home for several months while his family cared for him. With some trial and error (which is to be expected), Ben's psychiatrist was able to find the right combination of medications to appropriately address his condition, and the symptoms began to be more manageable. Ben described the events that followed his return home:

> I have been so blessed by treatments, people, family, and children that my dreams were not crushed. Meeting Lydia and the fact that she accepted my illness as her own has been the biggest blessing of my life. Our eternal marriage more than anything has given me hope. I know how important she is to me. I don't have to be alone now or ever again. I shouldn't forget to mention my kids. I realize the risk of having children and passing along my illness to them; maybe it is reckless of me, but having them is the second-best thing in my life. They fill me with joy. My

family is the reason I get up and go to work. They are the reason I do all that I do. I want them to be happy, and that gives me purpose in life.[15]

Ben is one of the kindest, most intelligent, and most pleasant people I know. Ben, Lydia, and their children are a faithful and caring family. Their love of God, love for one another, and love for their neighbors—including those who are considered different than others—are remarkable. Ben and his family continue to live with the reality of Ben's mental illness, but doing so has helped them become the wonderful people they are. Even by sharing his story with me, Ben's affliction with schizophrenia is being consecrated for his gain and for the gain and good of his family and friends.[16]

Schizophrenia and other psychotic disorders are among the most serious mental illnesses known to humankind. Even though a physician can detect various forms of cancer using an MRI or identify bacterial or viral infections through laboratory tests, schizophrenia and other related mental illnesses, including depression and anxiety, cannot be identified in the same ways. While scientists, psychiatrists, psychologists, and other mental health professionals continue to study and provide treatments for these disorders, we are in the early stages of finding the answers we seek. Chapters 5 and 6 provide more detail concerning the clinical and spiritual treatments of these disorders. As Latter-day Saints, we are also blessed to have the restored gospel of Jesus Christ to help us understand why God allows sickness, disease, and disability in our lives and how we can best face these adversities and afflictions.[17]

CHAPTER 4

PARENTS, CHILDREN, AND MENTAL HEALTH

"Bring up your children
in light and truth."
—*Doctrine and Covenants 93:40*

Dr. Carlfred Broderick (1932–1999)—a former professor of marriage and family therapy at the University of Southern California (USC), stake president, patriarch, and regular guest on the late-night Johnny Carson show—once illustrated how having an inspired understanding of the character of God and the doctrine of The Church of Jesus Christ of Latter-day Saints can lead to emotional healing.

Dr. Broderick's case study began when he referred a Latter-day Saint family to a Jewish colleague for family therapy. The parents initially resisted the therapist's counsel to "lighten up a little" in regard to the problems their teenage daughter was giving them, so the therapist sought Dr. Broderick's counsel: "This kid is about to run away from home or attempt suicide or do something else drastic," the therapist reported, "but, every time I suggest any movement in the direction of loosening up, they [the parents] patiently explain to me that I just don't understand their religious obligation, as Mormon parents, to keep this kid in line. Frankly, I don't know how to deal with this. I don't want to attack their religious beliefs, but the situation is explosive."

After some discussion, Dr. Broderick suggested a strategy in which the therapist would express interest in the family's religious beliefs, specifically in "the war in heaven." The therapist followed Dr. Broderick's suggestion. Shortly thereafter, he called and expressed gratitude and amazement at how well the counsel had worked. Dr. Broderick's colleague indicated that even the rebellious teen had offered to share with him "a copy of a book about their faith with a picture of their family in the front." The therapist was most surprised by the mother's dramatic change. She had responded quickly at the opportunity to share her beliefs [about the war in heaven], but her enthusiasm came to an end as quickly as it had started. The therapist described to Dr. Broderick what had happened: "In seconds she [the mother] had launched into some story about a council in heaven and two plans and she gets about three minutes into it and she stops cold in her tracks and gives me a funny look and says, 'All right, Doctor, you've made your point.' From that moment on they were like putty in my hands. It was like magic. Carl, what is this war in heaven?"[1]

The mother had suddenly (and humbly) realized that what she was doing in the name of her religious beliefs to control her daughter's behavior was similar to the strategy designed by the adversary to enslave the sons and daughters of God. Similar to how Satan attempted to "destroy the agency of man" (Moses 4:3), she was attempting to destroy the agency of her daughter by forcing her to follow the mother's dictates and meet her expectations.

While many, if not most, Latter-day Saints understand that Satan's intent was to selfishly force the children of God to do right, Professor Robert J. Matthews (1926–2009), former dean of Religious Education at BYU, described Lucifer's strategy differently:

> It seems strange to me that a third of all the spirits that had the potential to be born into this world would have favored a plan based on forced obedience. Most of us do not like to be forced. As I see it, the real issue was not so much one of force as it was that Lucifer said he would guarantee salvation for his spirit brothers and sisters. He promised

salvation without excellence, without effort, without hard work, without individual responsibility. That is the lie he promulgated in the preearth councils. That so-called shortcut to salvation captivated many gullible and lazy spirits. They wanted something for nothing.[2]

Whether Lucifer's plan was one of authoritarian power (as is generally taught), permissive indulgence (as Dean Matthews suggested), or both, the scriptures plainly teach that the adversary was and is "a liar from the beginning" (D&C 93:25) and that he "will not support his children at the last day, but doth speedily drag them down to hell" (Alma 30:60) by any means possible. While *authoritarian* parenting is more likely to be associated with emotional disturbance in children, research has shown that *permissive* parenting can also negatively influence children and adolescents.[3] The intent of this chapter is to provide examples of how parents can contribute to the emotional well-being of their children.

As children become adolescents and then young adults, parents often find balancing justice and mercy more complicated. In the October 2009 general conference, President Dallin H. Oaks provided the following counsel to parents with an unmarried adult child living with his or her partner and having sexual relations: "If an adult child is living in cohabitation, does the seriousness of sexual relations outside the bonds of marriage require that this child feel the full weight of family disapproval by being excluded from any family contacts, or does parental love require that the fact of cohabitation be ignored? *I have seen both of these extremes, and I believe that both are inappropriate.*"[4] President Oaks continued his comments by wisely counseling that how parents should respond in such a situation "is a matter for parental wisdom, guided by the inspiration of the Lord."

Parenting Styles

The relationship between parent and child is a key factor in mental and emotional health. Research studies often include the term *authoritarian* to describe a parenting style that is insensitive and rule bound. A parenting style that allows children to do as they please and provides minimal direction is described as *permissive*. A number of studies report that "young people growing up in families characterized by authoritarian and/or permissive behavior, establish insecure emotional relationships" and have an increased risk of mental health concerns, including suicide and depression.[5]

Authoritarian parenting has been shown to increase suicide risk among young men and young women who are members of the Church.[6] In President Oaks's address, he warned that both *excluding* the family member and *ignoring* his or her troublesome actions are "extremes" that are "inappropriate." In other words, he invited us to be authoritative but not authoritarian, and supportive but not indulgent as we strive to love and serve our family and others. The scriptural terms *justice* and *mercy* have been helpful to me in better understanding what it means to be both authoritative and supportive in relationships with others. The Savior taught, "Justice . . . is the habitation of thy throne; and mercy shall go before thy face and have no end" (Moses 7:31).

The *authoritative* (just) parent is loving and kind, sets reasonable expectations and boundaries, follows through with consequences (both positive and negative), and is open to negotiation; his or her focus is on the development of the child. The *authoritarian* parent is coercive, hostile, shaming, demeaning, controlling, rigid, and rule bound; does not negotiate; and focuses on meeting his or her own needs.

The *permissive* parent is indulgent and neglectful and provides little direction or correction. Sometimes one parent is *permissive* in an attempt to counterbalance the other parent whom they perceive to be authoritarian. Permissive parents often refrain from setting boundaries and providing structure. They generally expect little from their children and rarely provide consequences for negative behavior.

The *supportive* (merciful) parent, like the *authoritative* parent, focuses on the growth of the child. The *supportive* parent encourages children to discover their own strengths, is forgiving and gracious, and allows children to make mistakes without berating them.[7] The following diagram compares these four distinct parenting styles. The ideal is parents who are both supportive and authoritative and who avoid the permissive and authoritarian extremes.

	SUPPORTIVE (Merciful)	AUTHORITATIVE (Just)	
PERMISSIVE			AUTHORITARIAN

Suicide Risk

The relationship between authoritarian and permissive styles of parenting is becoming increasingly important with respect to mental health in general and to suicide in particular. The US Center for Disease Control and Prevention (CDC) recently reported that suicide was the third leading cause of death in the United States for children ages ten to fourteen.[8] Suicide rates are especially high in the Intermountain West, with Utah having the seventh highest suicide rate for teenagers in the nation.[9] Interestingly, however, the CDC has also reported that suicidal thoughts and suicide attempts among young men and young women in Utah are significantly lower among those who are active participants in The Church of Jesus Christ of Latter-day Saints than those who are not active or who are not members of the Church.[10] While other studies confirm these results, any suicide, and the associated trauma for others, is tragic and deserves our best efforts to prevent.[11]

Another research study reports that Latter-day Saints who identify as gay report better mental health than non–Latter-day Saint LGB individuals. However, mental health scores, including those indicating a higher risk of suicide, are not as positive for LGB Latter-day Saints as they are for non-LGB members of the Church. (The acronym "LGB" is used instead of "LGBT" because of the lack of research on those identifying as transgender).[12] President M. Russell Ballard recently stated: "We believe that the core rights of citizenship should be protected for all people—for LGBT people, for people of all faiths, and for everyone else. In essence, this means fairness for all. . . . We condemn, in the strongest terms, bullying or harassment of any kind. Every person is a child of God. Everyone is entitled to love and respect."[13]

Among other organizations, the National Institute of Mental Health and The Church of Jesus Christ of Latter-day Saints have provided helpful resources for those dealing with the different dimensions of suicide.[14] The Church's website includes several excellent resources, including an insightful address from President Ballard entitled "Suicide: Some Things We Know, and Some Things We Do Not."[15]

The Character, Perfections, and Attributes of God

Understanding that God is neither authoritarian nor permissive but is perfectly just (authoritative) and perfectly merciful (supportive) relates to our personal happiness and to the happiness and health of those we love and serve. The Savior included the following phrase in a prayer He offered to His Father: "And this is life eternal, that they might know thee the only true God, and Jesus Christ, whom thou hast sent" (John 17:3). Regarding the character of God, Professor Richard Rice explained: "What we think of God and how we respond to Him are closely related. An inaccurate view of God can have disastrous effects on personal religious experience. We could never love a hostile, tyrannical being. . . . And we could not respect a mild, indulgent figure who never took us seriously. Our personal religious experience can be healthy only if we hold an adequate conception of God."[16]

Having a distorted view of God not only can have a "disastrous" influence on our personal religious life but also can be especially destructive on our interpersonal relationships, especially those with our children, spouse, and others we have the privilege to love and lead. The Prophet Joseph Smith taught:

It is necessary for us to have an understanding of God himself in the beginning. If we start right, it is easy to go right all the time; but if we start wrong, we may go wrong, and it will be a hard matter to get right. There are but a very few beings in the world who understand rightly the character of God. . . . If men do not comprehend the character of God, they do not comprehend themselves. . . . It is the first principle of the Gospel, to know for a certainty the character of God.[17]

President Heber C. Kimball, a counselor to Brigham Young in the First Presidency, described several of the attributes of God that many individuals outside and inside the Church of Jesus Christ don't comprehend: "I am perfectly satisfied that my Father and my God is a cheerful, pleasant, lively, good-natured Being. Why? Because I am cheerful, pleasant, lively, and good-natured when I have His Spirit. That is one reason why I know; and another is—the Lord said, through Joseph Smith, 'I delight in a glad heart and a cheerful countenance.' That arises from the perfection of His attributes; He is a jovial, lively person, and a beautiful man."[18]

President Kimball's description echoes the words of the prophet Enoch who described God as "merciful and kind forever" (Moses 7:30). Heber C. Kimball's words also dramatically contrast with the god described in the following statement by atheist and professor Richard Dawkins: "The God of the Old Testament is arguably the most unpleasant character in all fiction: jealous and proud of it; a petty, unjust, unforgiving control-freak; a vindictive, bloodthirsty ethnic cleanser; a misogynistic, homophobic, racist, infanticidal, genocidal, filicidal, pestilential, megalomaniacal, sadomasochistic, capriciously malevolent bully."[19]

The disparity between the statements of President Kimball and Richard Dawkins represents the wide gulf between varying beliefs throughout the world about the character of God. Professor Dawkins's caricature of God is why some among us have lost faith. Addressing the misunderstandings many people have concerning the nature of God, Elder Jeffrey R. Holland taught:

> I make my own heartfelt declaration of God our Eternal Father . . . because some in the contemporary world suffer from a distressing misconception of Him. Among these there is a tendency to feel distant from the Father, even estranged from Him, if they believe in Him at all. And if they do believe, many moderns say they might feel comfortable in the arms of Jesus, but they are uneasy contemplating the stern encounter of God. . . . I bear personal witness this day of a personal, living God, who knows our names, hears and answers prayers, and cherishes us eternally as children of His spirit. I testify that amidst the wondrously complex tasks inherent in the universe, He seeks our individual happiness and safety above all other godly concerns. We are created in His very image and likeness, and Jesus of Nazareth, His Only Begotten Son in the flesh, came to earth as the perfect mortal manifestation of His grandeur.[20]

President Dallin H. Oaks once taught that understanding the true nature of God and our divine relationship with Him is a "potent antidepressant."[21]

"The Queen of Heaven"

Another unique and meaningful doctrine of the restored gospel that relates to parents, children, and mental health is the doctrine of a Heavenly Mother. The existence of our Mother in Heaven was first introduced, at least in print, by William W. Phelps when he penned, "O Mormonism! Thy father is God, thy mother is the Queen of heaven."[22] Elder Erastus Snow, a member of the Quorum of the Twelve, spoke on the gender identity of God, explaining a doctrine that is unique to the teachings of the Restoration:

> "What," says one, "do you mean we should understand that Deity consists of man and woman?" Most certainly I do. . . . There can be no God except he is composed of the

> man and woman united, and there is not in all the eternities that exist, nor ever will be, a God in any other way. . . . There never was a God, and there never will be in all eternities, except they are made of these two component parts; a man and a woman; the male and the female.[23]

The doctrinal, relational, and gendered truth described by Elder Snow has forever changed how I understand the nature of God. When I read the word *God* in scriptural text, I find great meaning in knowing that the reference can include both Heavenly Father and Heavenly Mother and serves as a divine invitation for each of us to become like Them, whether we be male or female.[24] Knowing that we are literally a son or daughter of a Heavenly Father *and* Mother clarifies and strengthens our sense of both mortal and postmortal identity and potential.

In addition to scriptural teachings, the research literature demonstrates that there is a correspondence between the relationships we have with our earthly mothers and fathers and our relationship with God.[25] While Sigmund Freud (1856–1939), one of the founders of psychiatry, argued God was an illusion, simply a "projection" of a "need" for a powerful father figure,[26] there is strong evidence that our understanding of God's character and the nature of our relationship with Him relate to our mental, emotional, and spiritual well-being. Those with a "secure relationship with God" score higher on measures of mental health than individuals whose relationship with God is weak or doesn't exist.[27] The research literature on "attachment to God" also suggests that individuals with unreliable or unstable relationships with their parents are able to compensate for their less-than-nurturing relationships with their parents by developing an intimate relationship with God.[28]

Though such a scenario would never happen, if Heavenly Father were to change from being a merciful God to one who is indulgent, or from being just to vengeful, He would, in Alma's words, "cease to be God" (Alma 42:25; see also Morm. 9:19). The same can be said for parents and leaders in responsible positions of influence if they distort the divine relationship between justice and mercy—they will cease to have an influence for good in the lives of those they love and serve. Perhaps one of the greatest lessons of life is to learn to love as He loved and to strive to help our families and others to do the same.[29]

CHAPTER 5

HEALING THE BROKEN BRAIN

"The spirit and the body
are the soul of man."
—*Doctrine and Covenants 88:15*

On July 29, 1932, George H. Brimhall, former president of Brigham Young University, died at his home in Provo, Utah. President Brimhall was seventy-nine years old and had been burdened by serious health problems for many years; his death was not unexpected. The article in the *Provo Daily Herald* that announced his death, however, disturbed those who knew President Brimhall as an able administrator, inspiring educator, devoted Church leader, capable community leader, and loving husband and father. According to the announcement, "[His] death was evidently caused by a bullet from a rifle." The announcement continued with the following explanation: "Members of his family observed that he had grown discouraged lately and his restless spirit chafed under the long siege which had sapped his strength."[1] While it is possible the shooting was accidental, those closest to President Brimhall concluded that he had taken his own life. A disturbing and sobering ending to the life of a man who had done so much good for so many.

Commenting on the tragic death of President Brimhall, then Elder George Albert Smith, of the Quorum of the Twelve Apostles (see pages 13–17), shared the following during the deceased's memorial service: "He has gone home. Not to some obscure, undesirable place. He has been working for a place in the Celestial Kingdom. He has been seeking to have his name recorded in the Lamb's Book of Life. And I believe that if any man has accomplished that desirable thing, George H. Brimhall has accomplished it."[2]

The leaders of The Church of Jesus Christ of Latter-day Saints have never condoned suicide for any reason, but consistent with Elder Smith's statement, prophets past and present have addressed the issue with mercy and grace. A broader application of their words helps us understand other difficult subjects, including mental illness. President Thomas S. Monson once wrote the following to a grieving family: "It is my belief that one who ends his own life has become so mentally clouded—for whatever reason—that he is no longer accountable for his actions."[3] President M. Russell Ballard, while acknowledging the seriousness of suicide, wrote the following:

> I feel that the Lord also recognizes differences in intent and circumstances: Was the person who took his life mentally ill? Was he or she so deeply depressed as to be unbalanced or otherwise emotionally disturbed? Was the suicide a tragic, pitiful call for help that went unheeded too long or progressed faster than the victim intended? Did he or she somehow not understand the seriousness of the act? Was he or she suffering from a chemical imbalance that led to despair and a loss of self-control?[4]

In addition to the consoling counsel from these prophet leaders, their broader message is that the origins of mental illness and emotional suffering can't always be explained as an act of freewill for which the individual is responsible. This merciful uncertainty also applies to some of the psychological disorders and mental states discussed in previous chapters. The reality that we do not know more than we do about the origins and treatments of mental illness and emotional suffering is an invitation for each of us to follow the words of the Savior: "Judge not unrighteously, that ye be not judged; but judge righteous judgement" (JST Matt. 7:2). Such counsel can help us to be humble about what we do know and open minded and charitable about what we do not.

Agency and Law

A companion principle to the reality that we are not always responsible for our thoughts, feelings, actions, or illnesses is the protective principle of moral agency. Elder Neal A. Maxwell (1926–2004) once taught: "Of course our genes, circumstances, and environments matter very much, and they shape us significantly. Yet there remains an inner zone in which we are sovereign, unless we abdicate. In this zone lies the essence of our individuality and our personal accountability."[5] Elder Maxwell's statement is an instructive description of the relationship between the doctrine of *agency* (the freedom to act) and certain *laws*, or limitations of agency (being acted upon). While I believe we are "free to choose" (2 Ne. 2:27) as we navigate the challenges of life (including mental illness), I also believe there can be limitations to our ability "to act for [our]selves and not to be acted upon" (2 Ne. 2:26).

We read in the Doctrine and Covenants that "unto every kingdom is given a *law*; and unto every *law* there are certain *bounds* also and conditions" (D&C 88:38; emphasis added). President Dallin H. Oaks provided a simple example of these bounds and laws in a symposium address at Brigham Young University in 1989: "In the flesh we are subject to the physical law of gravity. If I should hang from the catwalk in the Marriott Center and release my grip, I would not be free to will myself into a soft landing. And I cannot choose to run through a brick wall."[6] An inspired understanding of the doctrine of agency, informed by the limitations of law, helps us understand what is and isn't possible with respect to the causes and cures of mental illness. The Lord has taught that as we follow His will, freedom will follow: "Then said Jesus to those Jews which believed on him, If ye continue in my word, then are ye my disciples indeed; and ye shall know the truth, and the truth shall make you free" (John 8:31–32). We can strengthen or weaken our agency by how we use this divine gift, but we must be aware some forms of mental illness and physical disability are outside the bounds of our agency.

Carol

There are many individuals with physical, emotional, and mental limitations that they did not cause and from which they will not be free until the Resurrection. For many years I have known a woman who fell out of the back of a truck when she was a child and suffered a traumatic brain injury.[7] While Carol was eventually able to care for herself and live a meaningful life for many years, the consequences of her accident affected her life in almost every way. She lost much of her ability to navigate interpersonal relationships and never married or was able to be gainfully employed.

Soon after Carol was injured, she worked with a physical therapist and mental health professional who wanted to institutionalize her, judging that she would never be capable of living independently. Later, Carol worked with other therapists who, in my judgment, made demands of her that were unsuitable given her limitations; they demanded she use agency she did not have and could not gain. To my knowledge, Carol never struggled with drug addiction, but one of her favorite quotations was the Serenity Prayer, made popular by proponents of Alcoholics Anonymous: "God, grant me serenity to accept the things I cannot change, courage to change the things I can, and wisdom to know the difference."[8] My life has been forever blessed by Carol's courage as I watched her wrestle with the tension between agency and the physical, mental, and emotional limitations imposed on her by her accident. I'm looking forward to seeing Carol in the Resurrection—free of her burdens and limitations.

The following diagram illustrates the divine tension between agency, law, and their counterfeits—indeterminism and determinism. We need to learn to identify, understand, and live "the law of the Lord" (Isa. 30:9), to exercise the "moral agency" (D&C 101:78) God has given, and to avoid the counterfeit philosophies of determinism and indeterminism:

```
        LAW           AGENCY
         |              |
─────────┼──────────────┼─────────
DETERMINISM            |    INDETERMINISM
```

Determinism and Indeterminism

If we misunderstand the doctrine of agency by taking it beyond its inspired meaning, purpose, and application the Lord intended, we are in danger of being deceived and damaged by the counterfeit philosophy of *indeterminism*, which includes the notion that we are totally free, without limitations preventing us from overcoming any obstacle or achieving any goal.[9] Those who embrace this false philosophy believe related ideas, such as "Whatever the mind can conceive and believe, the mind can achieve."[10] The Savior alluded to this false philosophy when he taught, "Which of you by taking thought can add one cubit unto his stature?" (Matt. 6:27).

Even though miracles do occur, the reality for Carol and for many others in similar situations is that no matter how faithful and hardworking they may be, or how much they embrace a positive mental attitude, they must learn to live with the reality of their afflictions and limitations.

On the other extreme, *determinism* is the false philosophy that *every* thought, feeling, and limitation we experience (including mental illness) and *every* act we perform are completely determined by forces outside of our control.[11] Those who support the philosophy of determinism believe moral agency, our ability to make deliberate choices, is an illusion. Prophets have taught, and many philosophers and clinicians support the idea, that the causes and cures of mental illness lie somewhere on a continuum between moral agency and the laws and bounds of mortality. The alternative explanations of determinism and indeterminism bring hopelessness to some and false hope to others.

The Spirit and the Body

In addition to doctrines of moral agency and the constraints of law, another valuable perspective of the restored gospel of Jesus Christ is the elevated status of the physical body in relationship to the spirit as part of our temporal and eternal identity. The Lord revealed through the Prophet Joseph Smith that "the spirit and the body are the soul of man" (D&C 88:15). And the Lord instructed President Joseph F. Smith that "the spirit and the body" must be united in order to "receive a fulness of joy" (D&C 138:17).

Many religions and philosophical traditions include beliefs about the human body that reflect the ancient philosopher Plato's (428–348 BC) belief that "the body is a source of endless trouble to us" and after "having got rid of the foolishness of the body we shall be pure."[12] Plato's philosophy is consistent with the description of God as being without "body, parts, and passions" and the view that children at birth are naturally evil.[13] Such beliefs are also consistent with the arguments of those who reject the literal resurrection of Jesus Christ.[14] While an increasing number of scholars, clergy, and lay Christians are distancing themselves from the belief in a literal resurrection of Jesus Christ, the leadership and general membership of The Church of Jesus Christ of Latter-day Saints continue to embrace the doctrines of the "infinite Atonement and literal Resurrection" of Jesus Christ.[15]

"The Father has a body of flesh and bones as tangible as man's; the Son also" (D&C 130:22). This doctrinal reality helps us understand that the major purpose of our spiritual birth and mortal creation is to become like our Heavenly Parents, in both body and spirit, and to live as They live. The unique relationship between our spiritual and physical selves helps us better understand how mental and emotional disorders come about, how they can be managed, and in many cases how they can be overcome through psychological, medical, and spiritual interventions.

Psychological, Medical, and Spiritual Healing

I often feel sad when I meet with people who are clearly in need of help from well-trained therapists and knowledgeable and sensitive physicians but who insist that their mental health concerns can be resolved through more diligent discipleship. President George H. Brimhall, discussed earlier in this chapter, died well before psychotherapy was generally available and psychiatric medications were discovered, but his life might have been much different had he lived at a time when such resources were available. While I do not believe psychiatric medications are always the "miracle cure" some mental health providers and pharmaceutical companies would have the public believe,[16] such medical treatment may have provided him with significant relief.[17] President Brimhall was a man of great faith, and with the right psychological and pharmacological care, his depression might have been relieved and his death prevented. I find it instructive that the Book of Mormon includes examples of healing by priesthood power (see Alma 15:5–11), by studying and teaching "the word of God" (Alma 31:5), and by the use of the "many plants and roots which God had prepared to remove the cause of diseases" (Alma 46:40). While I admit my own skepticism concerning herbal cures that lack scientific validation, I also acknowledge that plants and roots are the origin of many of the proven medications in use today.[18]

Similar to the Savior's and His latter-day servants' teachings on the importance of both the spirit and the body, Latter-day Saint theology includes both sacred and secular truth. Healing can come through priesthood power and personal and prophetic revelation, as well as through clinical interventions. President Hugh B. Brown (1883–1975) once taught: "The Church of Jesus Christ of Latter-day Saints accepts newly revealed truth, whether it comes through direct revelation or from study and research. We deny the common conception of reality that distinguishes radically between the natural and the supernatural, between the temporal and the eternal, between the sacred and the secular."[19] The disorders we face and the healing we seek can be influenced by our spirit and our body, as well as by the sacred and the secular worlds in which we live.

My heart also aches when I meet with individuals whose psychological suffering appears to be, at least in part, linked to sin and/or transgression but who resist both the *redemptive* and *enabling* powers of Jesus Christ, made available through repentance. Elder David A. Bednar once taught: "It is one thing to know that Jesus Christ came to earth to die for us. . . . But we also need to appreciate that the Lord desires, through His Atonement and by the power of the Holy Ghost, to live in us—not only to direct us but also to empower us."

Elder Bednar's remarks illustrate two dimensions of what the Book of Mormon prophet Jacob described as the "infinite atonement" (2 Ne. 9:7). Elder Bednar continued his remarks by reminding us that we are not alone in facing our afflictions: "I frankly do not think many of us 'get it' concerning this *enabling* and *strengthening* aspect of the Atonement, and I wonder if we mistakenly believe we must make the journey from good to better and become a saint all by ourselves through sheer grit, willpower, and discipline, and with our obviously limited capacities."[20]

President Dallin H. Oaks taught something similar when he said, "For many, the infirmity of depression is painful or permanently disabling. . . . Those who suffer this circumstance should remember that our Savior experienced this kind of pain also and that, through His Atonement, He offers the strength to bear it."[21]

Counseling and Psychotherapy

Working with a psychologist or other licensed mental health professional can be an effective resource for those who are suffering as they seek solutions to their mental and emotional concerns. Elder Jeffrey R. Holland counseled: "Seek the advice of reputable people with certified training, professional skills, and good values. Be honest with them about your history and your struggles. Prayerfully and responsibly consider the counsel they give and the solutions they prescribe. If you had appendicitis, God would expect you to seek a priesthood blessing and get the best medical care available. So too with emotional disorders. Our Father in Heaven expects us to use all of the marvelous gifts He has provided in this glorious dispensation."[22]

While people should choose treatment options cautiously, the "marvelous gifts" Elder Holland spoke of could very well include both psychotherapy and medication; I have observed that the lives of many individuals have been blessed by both. The American Psychological Association has stated, "There is some evidence that combining psychotherapy and medications may be more effective than either treatment alone."[23]

Elder Alexander B. Morrison (1930–2018), an emeritus member of the Seventy and a university professor trained in nutrition and pharmacology, shared the following counsel: "Talk therapy, in which the patient begins to understand why he or she thinks and acts in certain ways and learns effective coping behavior, in order not just to avoid psychic pain but to overcome it, remains of vital importance in dealing effectively with mental illness." Elder Morrison continued by calling attention to the effectiveness of both medication and counseling:

> We should not underestimate the effectiveness of medication, which has helped untold millions of those with mental illness to come back to reality, overcome despair, regain hope, quell their inner demons, and live useful and productive lives. It seems to me that we are not dealing with a black-and-white situation, despite the debates about medication versus psychotherapy that continue to swirl and eddy throughout the community of mental health professionals. It seems obvious that both medication and psychotherapy have invaluable roles to play.[24]

A review of the research reveals that "more than 5,000 individual studies . . . have been conducted on the effectiveness of psychotherapy; these studies demonstrate that well-developed therapy interventions have meaningful, positive effects. . . . In short, not only does psychotherapy work, but research demonstrates that therapy is remarkably effective."[25]

Possible Reasons to Engage in Therapy

Mental illness and emotional disorders can have a profound effect on an individual's and family's quality of life and ability to function normally. Some of the reasons you might consider engaging in therapy include

- "Overwhelming sadness or helplessness that doesn't go away
- "Serious, unusual insomnia or sleeping too much
- "Difficulty focusing on work, or carrying out other everyday activities
- "Constant worry and anxiety
- "Drinking to excess or any behavior that harms self or others
- "Dealing with a difficult transition, such as a divorce, children leaving home, job difficulties, or the death of someone close
- "Children's behavior problems that interfere with school, family, or peers."[26]

Choosing a Therapist

Several years ago, one of my daughters returned home early from her mission because of problems she was having with anxiety and depression. As she was preparing to return home, I began my search for a therapist who could help her with her concerns. To reap the most benefits from psychotherapy, choosing a therapist should be done carefully. Influenced by my own training as a psychologist, I had some sense of what was needed. The general qualifications of the mental health professional I was looking for are summarized in the following statement from Elder Richard L. Evans (1906–1971), a former member of the Quorum of the Twelve Apostles: "It is a wonderful thing to be faithful, but a much greater thing to be *both faithful and competent*."[27]

Among those I considered to be my daughter's therapist were men and women who were faithful members of the Church but, in my judgment, hadn't received the necessary training or experience to be professionally competent. On the other hand, some of the most competent mental health professionals I considered were very well trained, but in my opinion, they weren't as faithful in the ways I believed were necessary to help my daughter. They often criticized the leaders of the Church and often put themselves and their ideas above prophetic counsel.

The therapist I was looking for would be a person of faith but who was not simply a member of The Church of Jesus Christ of Latter-day Saints. I was looking for a professional whose faith was grounded in the Savior and the teachings of the Savior's servants. I also wanted a therapist who was well informed by his or her intellect, well trained, and possessed a deep love and compassion for others—especially those who are suffering. It is also important to note that there are many mental health professionals around the world who, while not members of the Church, are both faithful and competent.

My decision about a therapist's competence often depends on my discussions with them concerning their philosophy of "cause and cure," reading articles and books they may have written, talking to other therapists who know and have worked with them, and, if possible, learning what their former clients have said about the care they have provided. In the process of looking for a therapist for my daughter, I asked my students and colleagues if they had had experiences with therapists who they would recommend. In addition to being prayerful and counseling with my wife, I also asked my Church leaders (both men and women) whom they had found helpful in similar circumstances. Choosing a therapist is something never to be taken lightly—all therapists are not created equal. I also explained to my daughter that if she didn't feel comfortable with the person I had identified, we would keep looking until we found someone she did. A good relationship between therapist and client is vital to therapeutic success.[28]

We found a faithful and competent therapist who was an employee of Family Services, an agency sponsored by the Church.[29] My daughter was greatly blessed to work with this faithful, kind, and competent man for several months and credits him with helping her work through her anxiety and depression. She was especially impressed with the compassion and empathy her therapist had developed through working with his own daughter who was suffering with cancer. The following is a summary of recommendations for choosing a therapist:

1. Be prayerful in your search. Make sure you have a sense of peace and confidence in working with the therapist you choose, even when what they say and recommend challenges your own thoughts and actions. A good therapist won't always tell you what you may want to hear.
2. Ask trusted friends, family, and Church leaders (men and women) for their recommendations.
3. Make sure your therapist will be respectful of your religious beliefs. Be especially cautious of therapists who want to "save you" from religion and the Church.
4. Verify that your therapist is well trained. This begins with her or him having a graduate degree from an accredited university and having experience working with your specific concern. Please remember, even though the mental health professional you are considering has an advanced degree (MD, PhD, MSW, LCSW), the degree itself doesn't make him or her a competent therapist. Your relationship with your therapist is vital.
5. Identify what kind of professional you are looking for. The term *therapist* usually describes one who has professional training to treat mental illness. A therapist can be a *psychologist* (who generally has a doctoral degree), a *clinical social worker* or *mental health counselor*

(who have master's degrees), or a *marriage and family therapist* (who can have a doctoral and/or a master's degree). A *psychiatrist* is a medical doctor (MD or DO) who has advanced training in the medical treatment of mental disorders (including the use of medication). Life coaches do not always have an academic or clinical degree and focus more on helping people achieve personal, family, or professional goals.

6. Verify that your therapist or physician is licensed in the state and nation in which you live.
7. Read what your prospective therapist has written about themselves and the work they do. Many therapists work as a part of larger practices that have websites with biographical descriptions.
8. Consider the gender of your therapist. Determine if working with a man or a woman would be best for you.
9. Consider speaking to the therapist on the phone or in person before you schedule an appointment.
10. Discuss payment and insurance options with your insurance company and the therapist before your first appointment.[30]

Bishops, stake presidents, Relief Society presidents, and other leaders of The Church of Jesus Christ of Latter-day Saints—though not a substitute for mental health professionals—can also provide valuable counsel. Some of the best outcomes I have observed have been when patient, therapist, and Church leaders all work together to address the needs of the individual or family.[31] As a stake president I was often amazed at the miracles I observed as faithful and competent bishops and Relief Society presidents magnified their priesthood power to bless the lives of those whom they loved and served.

Taking Medication

The right medication(s) matched with the right person and disorder can be helpful, but the reasons why they are effective are not always well understood.[32] Elder Alexander Morrison wrote the following concerning the cause and treatment of depression: "It does seem certain that one cannot fully explain depression by hypothesizing that it is caused simply by low brain levels of neurotransmitters and can therefore effectively be treated by increasing neurotransmitter levels by use of drugs. Whatever is happening at a cellular level during antidepressant therapy appears to be more complicated."[33]

The idea that the cause and the cure of depression is more complicated than the simple explanation of a "chemical imbalance" is especially important. To believe otherwise may leave the actual origin and solution to the problem unidentified. Various expressions of mental illness have been linked with a myriad of external factors including stressful life events such as death, divorce, unemployment, and physical illness. Other factors include cultural, spiritual, and religious influences; genetics; diet; education; spiritual, emotional, and physical trauma; brain tumors and lesions; and interpersonal conflicts in marriage, family, and work—to name only a few.[34] Helping their clients determine the causes and cures of their specific problems is the real work of faithful and competent professionals. Be wary of those with simplistic or quick answers who don't take the time to sincerely listen to your concerns.

Those considering taking medication also need to be aware that it isn't unusual for the medical professional who is prescribing the medication to experiment with different kinds of medications and different dosages before finding the right match. Medications can also take several weeks before a patient experiences any change. Be cautious of those who take either extreme, by either maligning medication or insisting that it is the only legitimate cure to be considered.

Depending on what is prescribed, medications can often have several side effects that accompany their use. The National Institute of Mental Health has an excellent website that describes the various medications used for different disorders and their possible side effects, which can include nausea and vomiting, weight gain, diarrhea, sleepiness, sexual dysfunction, etc.[35] Sometimes the expected "cure" can be worse than the disease. Communicate with the professionals with whom you are working; help them understand your concerns and how your healing is progressing or regressing.

Theories and Therapies of Change

Different mental health professionals have varying beliefs about how to best facilitate the changes both they and their clients hope to observe and to experience. A therapist's goal is to assist their clients in living healthier, happier, and more productive lives. Therapy can be delivered in the form of talk therapy (individual or group), psychiatric medication, or both.

While there are nearly as many theories of therapy as there are therapists, each theoretical perspective serves as a guide to help the therapist understand their client, identify the problems that need to be addressed, and work with the client to develop solutions. Examples of these therapies include the following:

- **Adlerian therapy** (Alfred Adler): Adlerian therapy is designed to help a client understand and challenge the goals of their (or other's) behavior: A = attention getting, B = bossing, C = counterhurting (hurting others before they hurt us), and D = disabling (to prove to others their inability to achieve).
- **Behavior therapy** (B. F. Skinner): The goal is to extinguish dysfunctional behavior and learn more functional behaviors that will help clients set and achieve goals. Behavioral therapy is especially helpful in overcoming phobias.
- **Cognitive behavior therapy—CBT** (Aaron Beck): CBT helps clients identify, refute, and correct cognitive distortions. Clients learn to identify the following: A = activating events, B = beliefs that are faulty and functional, C = consequences of beliefs, and D = distorted or irrational beliefs. This therapy identifies individual strengths, considers the

lives the clients would like to have, and helps them achieve rational expectations.

- **Existential therapy** (Viktor Frankl): This therapy was created to help clients develop a sense of freedom and personal responsibility. Clients are helped to identify obstacles that limit their freedom of thoughts, feelings, and actions.
- **Family systems therapy** (Murray Bowen): Family systems therapy aims to help families and individuals understand the influence of the family on individual behavior and how dysfunctional dynamics can exist across generations. Its goal is to create new and healthy ways of relating with a family or system.
- **Person-centered therapy** (Carl Rogers): The goal of person-centered therapy is to provide a setting of "unconditional positive regard," where clients are provided a safe and welcoming environment and are helped to develop confidence by finding answers to their problems and by becoming more self-directed.
- **Reality therapy** (William Glasser): This therapy helps clients learn to choose and accept responsibility for their behavior and accomplish their goals.[36]

Some therapists follow one of these theoretical perspectives as they work with clients, while others take an eclectic approach to therapy, which means they take the best from the various theories to meet the needs of their clients. In addition to in-session discussions, some therapists provide their clients with homework, which may include reading, writing, and practicing new ways of thinking, while others do not. Some therapists also include group therapy as a part of their treatment plan.

I am grateful for a divine plan that includes family, friends, Church leaders, helping professionals, and the miracles of modern science. President Hugh B. Brown (1883–1975) once taught: "Unlike those whose religious faith is uneasy and precarious in the modern world of expanding scientific knowledge, we are at home with the most advanced truths discovered by scientists and with all competent philosophic thought—with truth wherever found."[37] Above all else, we can be grateful for an almighty and all-loving God, who loves His children and who sent His Son to redeem us from our fallen state. President Dallin H. Oaks recently said: "Whatever the causes of large increases in anxiety and associated mental health diagnoses, our first line of defense is always our faith in the Lord Jesus Christ. We trust in His promises of peace and in the cleansing that His Atonement makes possible. Instead of being swept along in the anxiety and fear . . . , rely on the assurances of a loving Heavenly Father."[38] Broken brains, disordered minds, and broken hearts can be healed as we turn to Him and the multitude and variety of blessings He has made possible.

CHAPTER 6

HEALING THE BROKEN HEART

"And Jesus went about . . . healing every
sickness and every disease among the people."
—Matthew 9:35

During His ministry among the ancient inhabitants of the Americas, Jesus Christ, the "Savior of the world" (1 Ne. 13:40; John 4:42), made the following invitation: "Have ye any that are sick among you? Bring them hither. Have ye any that are lame, or blind, or halt, or maimed, or leprous, or that are withered, or that are deaf, or that are afflicted in any manner? Bring them hither and I will heal them, for I have compassion upon you; my bowels are filled with mercy" (3 Ne. 17:7).

In response to the Savior's invitation, "all the multitude . . . did go forth with their sick and their afflicted, and their lame, and with their blind, and with their dumb, and with all them that were *afflicted in any manner*; and he did heal them every one" (3 Ne. 17:9; emphasis added). The Savior's words "afflicted in any manner" suggest that in addition to healing those with physical infirmities, He also healed those with spiritual, mental, and emotional afflictions.

Though the account in 3 Nephi doesn't include the specific identities of those whom the Savior healed, the text does reveal that the number of those in attendance during this particular day of His ministry among them was "about two thousand and five hundred souls . . . consist[ing] of men, women, and children" (3 Ne. 17:25). Twenty-five hundred people is nearly the size of one of the districts or the "stakes of Zion" (D&C 107:36) of The Church of Jesus Christ of Latter-day Saints that have been established throughout the world. Emphasizing the Savior's love for each individual, this account also includes the significant detail that "the multitude went forth . . . and did feel the prints of the nails in his hands and in his feet; and this they did do, going forth *one by one* until they had all gone forth . . . and did know of a surety and did bear record, that it was he, of whom it was written by the prophets, that should come" (3 Ne. 11:15; emphasis added). The most important knowledge we can gain in this world or the next is that Jesus Christ is the Savior and Redeemer of every man, woman, and child—collectively and individually. President Gordon B. Hinckley once taught: "With all of our doing, with all of our leading, with all of our teaching, the most important thing we can do for those whom we lead is to cultivate in their hearts a living, vital, vibrant testimony and knowledge of the Son of God, Jesus Christ. . . . Whenever a man has a true witness in his heart of the living reality of the Lord Jesus Christ all else will come together as it should."[1]

Spiritual Solutions

Building on the pioneering work of one of our early mentors, Professor Allen E. Bergin, I joined with two of my colleagues, Professors P. Scott Richards and G. E. Kawika Allen, in leading a worldwide research initiative focusing on the effectiveness of spiritual- and religious-oriented psychotherapies. Our research team included 19 separate groups including clinicians, researchers, and clergy from 7 different faith traditions and 11 disciplines. Our research teams included clinicians and researchers from North, Central, and South America; Asia; the Middle East; Europe; and the South Pacific. We collected data from 300 healthcare professionals, 9,000 clients, and 32,000 psychotherapy sessions conducted over the course of nearly 3 years.[2] This extraordinary group of clinicians, clients, clergy, and scholars define religion and spirituality and understand God in different ways, but we all agree that there is a God who loves His children and wants to heal them of their afflictions.

Even though we are in the early stages of analyzing the results of what may be the largest study of this kind ever to be conducted, we can safely conclude that faith in God and religious belief and practice has demonstrated clinical power to "heal the broken hearted" and "set at liberty them that are bruised" (Luke 4:18; see also Psalm 147:3; and Yunus 10:57 [of the Quran]).[3]

"How Is It Done?"

As Latter-day Saints, we often hear that the Atonement of Jesus Christ can heal us of our afflictions, but many have the same question the young Enos asked of the Lord: "how is it done?" (Enos 1:7). While it would be presumptuous to say that any mortal can provide complete answers to this difficult question, the remainder of this chapter includes information and recommendations that can help you respond to this most important question for yourself and that can help you assist those you love and serve. This particular chapter includes examples and suggestions from the lives of individuals who have struggled with depression and anxiety and learned to successfully live peaceful, productive, and meaningful lives. You will notice both similarities and differences among the various accounts because people's experiences with mental illness are rarely the same.

Alyssa

A good friend and colleague, whom I will call Alyssa (not her real name), recently shared with me a brief account of her experiences with anxiety and depression that illustrates many of the points found in the previous chapters:

> I was sure that if I just read my scriptures and prayed more, the depression would be removed, and yet it was not. The more I did, the less I felt of the Spirit. After trying multiple different anti-depressants and numerous visits with a psychiatrist [over the course of 1½ years],

the deepness of the depression finally lifted slightly, just enough that I felt a hint of revelation, which prompted me to go to the temple, 4½ hours away. Not an easy thing to do with three small children, no family nearby to help, and not feeling I could confide in friends or other members of the Church. With the support of my husband, we found a way. After thoughtful worship and heartfelt prayer, while there in the celestial room of the temple, I felt an overwhelming love from the Lord come over me, which filled me with peace and instantly, miraculously broke the grip that the depression had on me. From that moment, I began to heal, and within a fairly short amount of time, I was functional again and haven't relapsed since. It was a witness to me of the enabling power of Christ's grace and the healing power of His Atonement and how, conversely, sometimes we are completely powerless to effect a change ourselves, no matter how obedient or diligent we are, whether in large or small ways.[4]

Alyssa is an example of the Lord's promise that He will "ease the burdens which are put upon [our] shoulders." She also exemplifies one who is following the Savior's direction to "stand as witnesses for me hereafter, and that ye may know of a surety that I, the Lord God, do visit my people in their afflictions" (Mosiah 24:14).

One of the insights Alyssa's account includes is that even though she was a faithful member of the Church, she had reached a point in her discipleship that the more she read the scriptures and prayed, the less she felt the presence of the Spirit. At least some of Alyssa's concerns were similar to those described by Martin Luther (confusion over obedience and grace—see chapter 2), but she may also have been experiencing what the Savior described when He taught that it is possible to be "baptized with fire and with the Holy Ghost, and . . . [know] it not" (3 Ne. 9:20; see also Ether 12:14). While Alyssa may have been worthy of the presence of the Spirit, the depression she was experiencing may have been what was preventing her from feeling the peace and direction she was seeking, no matter how much she tried to be obedient.

Thousands of studies have been done that report the positive influence of religion and spirituality on mental health, but very few exist that describe the reverse—the negative influence of mental illness on an individual's religious and spiritual beliefs and experiences. As Alyssa experienced, not being able to feel the presence of the Spirit as they once had is one of the concerns I hear most often from active and faithful Latter-day Saints who are experiencing feelings of depression.

Ironically, another reason some people may not feel the presence of the Spirit could be the side effects of the antidepressant medications they are taking. Research studies report "emerging evidence that, in some individuals, persistent use of antidepressants may be pro-depressant."[5] In other words, some antidepressants create rather than relieve depression—they become part of the problem rather than the cure.

Alyssa's story, however, also illustrates that some antidepressant medications can be an important part of a cure. Prior to her experience in the temple, Alyssa had been working with a psychiatrist who, in addition to providing psychotherapy, worked with her to find the right medication that would eventually help prepare her to receive and recognize the spiritual prompting that eventually led to her being free of depression and anxiety. Sometimes, the appropriate medication can help prepare the way for spiritual, psychological, and physical healing.

In Alyssa's case, the right medication and psychotherapy were very helpful, but they weren't the only solutions to her depression and anxiety. After being on medication for a time, Alyssa reported feeling "a hint of revelation, which prompted [her] to go to the temple." In the temple she "felt an overwhelming love from the Lord," which lifted her depression.[6] When I first read Alyssa's account, I thought of the words of the prophet Jonah when he cried from "out of the belly of hell. . . . I am cast out of thy sight; yet I will look again toward thy holy temple" (Jonah 2:2, 4). Alyssa recently shared the following free-verse poem, entitled "In the Wilderness," to describe her experience with being delivered from depression:

> *Lost in a maze of confusion*
> *I wander—*
> *not knowing what to think,*
> *who to believe.*
>
> *Afloat in a sea of discouragement,*
> *I am tossed—*
> *riddled with self-doubt:*
> *Who am I? Am I of worth?*
>
> *From a dark mist of despair*
> *I cry for help,*
> *for strength.*
> *Then I feel the arms of a loving Father*
> *and hear His voice, saying,*
> *"My child, my daughter, I am here always. These*
>   *things are for you to learn, to grow, to become.*
> *Talk, I will listen. Ask, I will help. Cry, I will*
>   *comfort. Always."*
> *Suddenly, out of the wilderness I emerge*
> *onto a shining pathway of hope.*[7]

Alyssa's story is an important example of the blessings of the Atonement of Jesus Christ and the power and peace that can be found in His holy house. While Alyssa's story includes a miraculous recovery not experienced by others in similar circumstances, her account is also a testament of how faith in God, joined with the resources of modern medicine and psychotherapy, can bring about miraculous healing.

Elder D. Todd Christofferson of the Quorum of the Twelve Apostles identified what I believe was the key that allowed Alyssa to access the power of God and the blessings of the Atonement of Jesus Christ: "What is the source of such moral and spiritual power, and how do we obtain it? The source is

God. Our access to that power is through our covenants with Him. A covenant is an agreement between God and man, an accord whose terms are set by God (see Bible Dictionary, "Covenant," 651). In these divine agreements, God binds Himself to sustain, sanctify, and exalt us in return for our commitment to serve Him and keep His commandments."[8]

While it is important to realize that the Savior intervenes "in his own time, and in his own way, and according to his own will" (D&C 88:68), honoring the covenants we make with God is vital in order to receive the healing blessings of the Atonement of Jesus Christ. Alyssa's story includes elements of many of these covenants, including obedience, sacrifice, striving to live the higher laws of the gospel, and consecrating her life to the Savior.

Being in a *covenant* relationship with God is much different than seeing our relationship with Him as a *contract*. A contract is based on the premise that if God holds up His end of the deal, we will hold up ours. Others, like Alyssa, understand that being in a covenant relationship with God means that we honestly strive to keep the covenants we have made, even when it seems we aren't receiving the promised blessings we seek (see Mal. 3:13–18). Striving to keep the covenants we make, most importantly to take upon ourselves the name of Jesus Christ and to keep His commandments, allows the enabling power of His Atonement to heal our minds and hearts. And sometimes keeping the covenants we have made with God means that we do less and not more, as illustrated by the next two stories.

Professor Robert L. Millet

The prophet Lehi promised his son Jacob, "Thou shalt dwell safely with thy brother, Nephi" (2 Ne. 2:3). The Lord raises up different people at different times to be a blessing in our lives. Personally, I could name many such men and women who have been a blessing to me, as Nephi was to Jacob—including my friend and fellow professor of ancient scripture, Robert L. Millet.

Several years ago, Brother Millet experienced for the first

time in his life what has been described in previous chapters as "major depressive disorder." Bob described the beginnings of his experience with depression and anxiety as follows:

> In October of 2000 I experienced something I had never undergone before—I went into a deep depression for several months. Oh, I had had a bad day here and there, had known frustration and disillusionment like everyone else, but I had never been trapped by the tentacles of clinical depression so severely that I simply could not be comforted and could not see the light at the end of the tunnel. For days at a time I only wanted to sleep or gaze at the walls or be alone. For weeks I felt as though I was in a closed casket, a prison cell that allowed no light or sound whatever.[9]

Bob did what many of us would do if we were faced with similar challenges—he prayed and studied the best he could, received priesthood blessings, and counseled with others who had experienced depression or anxiety. Bob also sought the advice of his physician, who described his condition as "depletion depression," the same description Elder Holland would use thirteen years later in his October 2013 general conference address.[10]

At the time Bob began to feel depressed and anxious, he was serving as a stake president and had recently finished a ten-year tenure as the dean of Religious Education at BYU. He described this period as "a time in my life when my body, my emotions, and my mind had chosen—whether I liked it or not—to take a vacation from normalcy. I had been driven for too long and could no longer live on adrenaline." The First Presidency and the Area Presidency to whom he reported as a stake president "tenderly and kindly encouraged" President Millet "to turn everything over to [his] counselors and take the needed break and follow the doctor's orders, including using . . . medication if prescribed."[11] President Millet "took the medication, and within several months the feelings of gloom and doom and helplessness gradually passed."[12] In a recent email, Bob shared with me his perspective on taking medication as a part of his treatment:

> I had no hesitation whatsoever in taking [medication] because I was convinced that I needed medical help for my condition, just as my father needed insulin for his diabetes and my mother needed help with her high blood pressure. . . . I have continued to take the meds for the last twenty years. I still have days when things seem darker, when the slightest task seems overwhelming, or when I find myself feeling emotionally down for a day or two. But I have decided that that's just the way life is. We simply don't have control over all the variables—conditions of a fallen world, including a body and mind that are moving toward death.[13]

Daniel K Judd

While my own "dark night of the soul" wasn't as severe as what Brother Millet has described, I too have experienced "depletion depression." After finishing graduate school in the late 1980s, my family and I moved from Provo, Utah, to Lansing, Michigan. My wife, Kaye, had just given birth to our third child, and I had started a new career as an institute teacher in the Church Educational System. I had also started a new practice as a psychologist, and I was serving as a bishop. My best guess is that many of those who read this book have experienced a time in their lives when they had nothing more to give. Paradoxically, I was having great success in most every part of my life, but at the same time I was feeling more and more helpless and hopeless each day.

My recovery included the care of a loving family; a confrontation by James Cotton, my high priests group leader at the time; and a couple of months in bed diagnosed with an autoimmune disease. Brother Cotton reminded me that our ward already had a Savior, and it wasn't me. He emphatically and lovingly demanded that I make better use of the many able leaders in our ward and stop trying to do it all on my own.

The most significant part of my healing came in the form of "bibliotherapy" as I was led to a new understanding of the Savior's words in the New Testament: "And whosoever shall compel thee to go a mile, go with him twain" (Matt. 5:41). During my convalescence I studied the textual differences between the King James Version and the Joseph Smith Translation of the Sermon on the Mount. I found one difference in particular that played a significant role in changing my life for the better:

KJV Matthew 5:41	JST Matthew 5:43
And whosoever shall compel thee to go a mile, go with him twain.	And whosoever shall compel thee to go a mile, go with him a mile; and whosoever shall compel thee to go with him twain, thou shalt go with him twain.

My first thought as I read the words of the Joseph Smith Translation version was that I had misread the text.[14] As I read and reread these verses, I sensed that I was being blessed with a hidden treasure of knowledge. The Joseph Smith Translation of Matthew 5:43 helped me understand that going the second mile in parts of my life where I should have been going only "a mile" was a major reason for my exhaustion and feelings of despair. I was doing what the prophet Jacob described as "looking beyond the mark" (Jacob 4:14). Sometimes, going the second mile is what the Lord asks of us, but other times, true discipleship means going only one mile, not two.

The feelings of anxiety and depression I was experiencing were invitations for me to reconsider being "careful and troubled about many things" (Luke 10:41). But like Martha, to whom these words were originally directed, I needed to learn to be more like Martha's sister Mary and follow the Savior's direction to seek the "good part." While Martha "was cumbered about much serving," Mary "sat at Jesus' feet, and heard his word." When Martha complained that her sister had left her alone to do all of the physical preparations for an upcoming meal, Jesus commended Martha for what she was doing but taught her that "one thing is needful: and Mary hath chosen that good part, which shall not be taken away from her." While it may have been commendable in the eyes of many for Martha (and me) to have been "careful and troubled about many things," other things were more "needful" (Luke 10:39–42). In my case (and perhaps Martha's), the "good part" was doing less and not more.

I am grateful to have learned from my anxiety and depression how to be a living (and healthy) witness of the truthfulness of the counsel given by President Boyd K. Packer when he taught, "True doctrine, understood, changes attitudes and behavior. The study of the doctrines of the gospel will improve behavior quicker than a study of behavior will improve behavior."[15] I credit this precious doctrinal understanding as being central to the eventual restoration of my health.

My personal experience with feelings of depression and anxiety was an opportunity to apply what I had been taught in my clinical training, to reframe these "dark emotions" as tutors and not necessarily as evidences of psychopathology. Psychotherapist Miriam Greenspan wrote: "A culture that insists on labeling suffering as pathology, that is ashamed of suffering as a sign of failure or inadequacy, a culture bent on the quick fix for emotional pain, inevitably ends up denying both the social and spiritual dimensions of our sorrows. . . . The emotions that appear to afflict us can be the vehicles of our liberation from suffering."[16]

Janice

Janice's story offers an example of someone whose mental and emotional burdens led her to remember and live the covenants she had made to "take upon" herself the name of Jesus Christ, to "always remember him and keep his commandments" (D&C 20:77).

I first met with Janice (not her real name) only hours after her husband had confronted her with his intention to end their marriage. Janice's husband had told her that he did not love her, he had never loved her, and their marriage had been a mistake from the beginning. Even though Janice knew that she and her husband had serious marital problems to work through, she thought they had been making progress. She was devastated by her husband's criticism, callousness, lack of commitment to work through their differences, and harsh demands for a divorce. Not only was Janice experiencing a hurt she described as coming from "deep within her soul" over what was happening with her marriage, she had also already been experiencing symptoms of depression (including thoughts of suicide), even before the confrontation with her husband.

After counseling with Janice and helping make arrangements for her to be hospitalized (because of her risk for suicide), I contacted her husband. He was a good man in many ways, but he had lost all compassion for his wife and had made his position very clear that he had no desire to reconcile. He was already moving forward with his plans to end their marriage. From what I understood, he wanted his wife to "just go away," believing he and his children would be better off without her. This perspective is especially troubling because it reinforces one of the most common beliefs that individuals who attempt suicide often embrace—the misconception that their family and friends are better off without them. Research studies and clinical observations alike identify "perceived burdensomeness and failed belongingness" as two of the most common reasons why people take their own lives.[17]

During the next few days after our first visit, many people came forward to assist Janice, including her parents, Church leaders, therapists, and good friends, but she continued to descend into a deep despair.[18] She was losing hope that she and her husband could reconcile and that she could continue to be the mother her children needed. I believed Janice could make it through the dark days ahead, but I worried that these difficult hours and days could turn into months and perhaps years.[19] The prognosis for people with depression and other forms of mental illness is actually quite good, but learning to manage and to heal from such conditions is often a long process.[20] Janice was hospitalized, received psychotherapy, worked extensively with her priesthood and Relief Society leaders, and was supported by friends and family. Even though she had good support, many of us were concerned about what might lay ahead for her and her family.

To my surprise, when I met with Janice ten days after our first visit, her countenance had changed dramatically for the better. Her manner was quiet and subdued, but I could see she had a strength that I had not seen before. During the first few minutes of our discussion, I mistakenly thought that Janice's husband had experienced a change of heart and that they were in the process of working through their differences. When I asked Janice how she was feeling, she explained that her relationship with her husband was actually worse than it had been the last time we met. She explained further that in addition to continuing with his plans for divorce, her estranged husband had messaged her through his attorney of his intent to petition for legal custody of their children.

I asked Janice how it was possible for her to be so peaceful and to have gained what appeared to me to be so much strength in such a short amount of time, even though her circumstances appeared to have become even more difficult. She explained to me that while she believed the counseling she was receiving from her therapist and Church leaders was helpful and her family and friends were being exceptionally supportive, she didn't completely understand her newfound strength. As we continued our conversation, Janice shared with me that the troubles she was facing in the present had helped her remember some of the profound lessons she had learned in the past. Our conversation eventually led to Janice sharing with me the familiar words of the prophet Helaman to his sons Nephi and Lehi:

> And now, my sons, remember, remember that it is upon the rock of our Redeemer, who is Christ, the Son of God, that ye must build your foundation; that when the devil shall send forth his mighty winds, yea, his shafts in the whirlwind, yea, when all his hail and his mighty storm shall beat upon you, it shall have no power over you to drag you down to the gulf of misery and endless wo, because of the rock upon which ye are built, which is a sure foundation, a foundation whereon if men build they cannot fall. (Hel. 5:12)

I had read the words of Helaman many times, but my conversation with Janice helped me have a better understanding of the beauty and power of the word of God (see Alma 31:5) to help heal "the wounded soul" (Jacob 2:8).

I have learned as a therapist and as a priesthood leader to be cautious of simplistic answers to complex problems. But as I carefully listened to Janice describe what she believed to be the best way forward, I sensed that while the answers she was finding to her problems were simple, they were also substantive. As she spoke, I also thought of the prophet Nephi's words when he recorded, "And because of the simpleness of the way, or the easiness of it, there were many who perished" (1 Ne. 17:41). While we do need to be cautious of simplistic answers that distract us from real problems and solutions, profound answers to complex problems can sometimes be simpler than we may suppose. I have also learned that complexity can be a distraction and in some cases why we do not move forward. Elder Neal A. Maxwell once taught:

> The simpleness, the easiness of the gospel is such that it causes people to perish because they can't receive it. We like variety. We like intellectual embroidery. We like complexity. We like complexity at times because it gives us an excuse for failure; that is, as you increase the complexity of a belief system, you provide more and more refuges for those who don't want to comply. You thereby increase the number of excuses that people can make for failure to

comply, and you create a sophisticated intellectual structure which causes people to talk about the gospel instead of doing it. But the gospel of Jesus Christ really is not complex. It strips us of any basic excuse for noncompliance, and yet many of us are forever trying to make it more complex.[21]

Janice explained that many years earlier, while serving as a missionary in a foreign country, she first began to understand and experience what it really meant to "take upon [her] the name of Jesus Christ" (D&C 20:37). As she struggled to learn a difficult language, live peacefully with difficult companions, and become the kind of missionary that could help make a difference in people's lives, she learned to make "feasting upon the word of Christ" (2 Ne. 31:20), and not simply reading her scriptures, a daily priority. She also learned the joy of repentance and the spiritual and intellectual sense of adventure that can come from seeking and striving to follow the promptings of the Holy Ghost. Her mission had been especially difficult, but her experiences helped her lay an inspired foundation she was now attempting to reestablish.

A couple of years after Janice returned home from her mission, she met and married her husband. She described him as having been loving and faithful, and she had believed he would be a wonderful husband and father. A year or so after they were sealed in the temple, they had their first child. During the next few years, things began to change. Like so many of us, with all the demands of marriage, employment, schooling, having children, etc., she was no longer praying with "real intent" (Moro. 10:4) and "feasting upon the pleasing word of God" (Jacob 2:9) as she had learned to do as a missionary. Without even being fully aware of what was happening, the foundation she had once established, built "upon the rock of our Redeemer" (Hel. 5:12), had shifted from the Savior to her family, work, and even the Church. Even though Janice understood that she had a difficult journey ahead, Helaman's familiar words helped her remember the strength and power she had once experienced as she built her life on the foundation of Jesus Christ. She was once again experiencing that same strength and power and had the conviction that, no matter what happened with her marriage and family, she knew "in whom [she] should trust" (Morm. 9:20).

Time and space won't allow me to share all of the details of what I observed Janice doing in the months and years that followed to reestablish her foundation in Christ and regain her spiritual strength, but one meaningful practice she shared with me will give you a sense of some of the changes she made in her life. Instead of allowing the cries of her youngest child to awaken her each morning, she became more deliberate about waking up on her own initiative. She made the decision "to act for [herself] and not to be acted upon" (2 Ne. 2:26) by setting and waking to her own alarm, getting out of bed, sliding to her knees and offering a prayer. This was Janice's way of reminding herself Who came first in her life. While she wasn't always able to pray and study first thing in the morning, she was deliberate in making the effort to follow this simple direction from a loving Savior.

The following promise made by the prophet Nephi is meaningful for anyone trying to find their way through difficult circumstances:

> Wherefore, I said unto you, feast upon the words of Christ; for behold, *the words of Christ will tell you all things what ye should do*. Wherefore, now after I have spoken these words, if ye cannot understand them it will be because ye ask not, neither do ye knock; wherefore, ye are not brought into the light, but must perish in the dark. For behold, again I say unto you that *if ye will enter in by the way, and receive the Holy Ghost, it will show unto you all things what ye should do*. (2 Ne. 32:3–5; emphasis added)

Janice's story is an important example of being open to divine guidance that included approaching concerns in a variety of different ways, including a recommitment to study and prayer and counseling from her priesthood leaders, physicians, and therapist.

One of the prophetic resources Janice credits with helping her through these difficult days was a general conference address given by President Ezra Taft Benson in 1986 entitled "Do Not Despair." The article includes the following principles for building a Christ-filled foundation:

> 1. Repentance (Moro. 10:22)
> 2. Prayer (D&C 136:29)
> 3. Service (Luke 9:24)
> 4. Work (Gen. 3:17)
> 5. Health (D&C 88:15, 124)
> 6. Reading (Jacob 2:8)
> 7. Blessings (James 5:14–15)
> 8. Fasting (Matt. 17:21)
> 9. Friends (D&C 88:133)
> 10. Music (1 Sam. 16:14–23)
> 11. Endurance (2 Ne. 31:20)
> 12. Goals (Philip. 3:14)[22]

Building our lives on the foundation of Jesus Christ assures us that even though we will face losses and disappointments, we will always have access to the peace and direction of the Lord. The prophet Isaiah taught: "For the mountains shall depart and the hills be removed, but my kindness shall not depart from thee, neither shall the covenant of my peace be removed, saith the Lord that hath mercy on thee" (3 Ne. 22:10). In other words, we may suffer great loss—the loss of love, the loss of a loved one, the loss of a dream, the loss of health, and so much more—but the Lord has promised that if we are true to the covenants we have made with Him, we can have the peace and the direction that comes through the influence of the Holy Ghost.

Even though Janice continued to strengthen her foundation in Christ, she and her husband eventually divorced. There have been difficult times since her marriage ended, but Janice has continued to gain spiritual and emotional strength in the years that have followed. Janice has since remarried and found joy in her new marriage and in rearing her children. Most importantly, she continues to live the covenant she made to take upon herself the name of Christ by continuing to place Him at the center of her life. She learned that by centering her life on the Savior, she is better able to love and serve her family and others. The following words from President Howard W. Hunter summarize the lesson we can learn from Janice's experiences: "If our lives and our faith are centered on Jesus Christ and his restored gospel, nothing can ever go permanently wrong. On the other hand, if our lives are not centered on the Savior and his teachings, no other success can ever be permanently right."[23]

CONCLUSION

> "For God hath not given us the spirit of fear; but of power, and of love, and of a sound mind."
> —2 Timothy 1:7

Personally, I have never experienced the depth of anxiety and depression that has been a part of the lives of those whose stories I have shared in the previous chapters. Neither have I experienced the complexity of confusion that often accompanies schizophrenia or other psychotic disorders. I haven't experienced the clinical expressions of any of these forms of mental illness or emotional disturbance, but I have spent much of my adult life working with and studying the lives of those who have. I feel an immense sense of gratitude for these remarkable men and women and their willingness to share their stories and allowing me to be a part of their lives.

As I studied the life of President George H. Brimhall (see chapter 5) and learned of the personal, familial, religious, academic, physical, and psychological tensions with which he lived, I experienced the same gratitude I felt for the others whose stories I have shared, but also a sense of brotherhood. I was especially interested to learn that Brother Brimhall served as a patriarch in his stake and as the dean of Religious Education at Brigham Young University, two responsibilities we share.[1]

There are many similarities between Brother Brimhall's life and the lives of many other dedicated Latter-day Saints

CONCLUSION

living in the decades since his death. He had once been in the "eye of the storm," with his large family, heavy university assignments, and service in the Church and community. Sadly, because of his physical and mental health concerns, this once extraordinarily productive and influential man spent the last few years of his life isolated from much of what his life had once been about.

I believe President Brimhall could have avoided such a tragic end to his life had he lived during a time when he would have had access to the blessings of the psychological and medical care we have today. I also believe that Brother Brimhall would have been blessed by the increased understanding of the strengthening as well as the redemptive blessings of the Atonement of Jesus Christ we as a Church have come to better understand these past few decades. He understood the restored gospel, but the fallenness of the mortal world in which he lived broke his heart and disordered his mind, preventing him from receiving the full blessings of the gospel until the Resurrection.

The following quotation describes a dream Brother Brimhall once had that he shared with Elder Orson F. Whitney of the Quorum of the Twelve Apostles. Brother Brimhall's account is evidence to me that he understood the power of the restored gospel, including the grace of Christ, to heal those who are suffering. On January 15, 1924, President Brimhall wrote the following letter during a time Elder Whitney was enduring serious health challenges of his own: "I can appreciate in part the fight you have had to make, for I have been on that front where the struggle was extended into years of, seemingly at times, single-handed combat, so far as human help was concerned. Many a sunset brought from me the inward exclamation, 'Thank God I'm one day nearer to the end,' the place where the road would turn."

Brother Brimhall continued by sharing the parts of his dream that strengthened him during his own times of loneliness, physical affliction, and despair:

And then I dreamed, or rather, God gave me comfort and courage thru a dream: I found myself on the western slope of Mount Timpanogos making my way thru deep snow toward the top. The wind blew my hat off and whipped my coat to shreds. So steep and slippery became the slope that I could not stand but crawled, clinging to the ice. I wore out my gloves, my finger nails and the flesh from off my finger tips. My shoes were full of holes and my overalls and trousers were frazzled half way to my knees. I dared not look back but did look upward and forward. I reached the top of one ice-slide to find myself facing another. My heart sank and but for the memory of what I had done I should have despaired. I resolved to climb on, to do my best, and leave the rest with the Lord, and then in my dream I was caught by some power invisible, except to the feelings, and literally lifted over the top to fields of flowers, forests of pine, and running brooks, and what was most wholly unexpected, a group of my brethren engaged in some constructive work.

President Brimhall concluded his experience with the following: "I awoke and resolved anew to fulfill the prediction of Apostle Owen Woodruff that I should get well and be of service when most men said, 'He is done for.' I said to myself, climb on for the Lord will lift you over when the crisis comes." Broken brains, broken bodies, and broken hearts can all heal; "by [His] grace . . . after all we can do" (2 Ne. 25:23). We too must do our part to "climb on for the Lord will lift [us] over when the crisis comes."[2]

Physical and emotional afflictions are experienced by "the learned, the wise and the noble" (D&C 58:10), "the weak and the simple" (D&C 1:23), and by those of us somewhere in between. Each of us, no matter who we are, are entitled to the blessings of God's love. My wife, Kaye Judd, wrote the following in the midst of health challenges she has been courageously enduring for several years:

CONCLUSION

There is much to be learned in stillness and suffering. I have found the Lord in new, beautiful, and personal ways. I know Him better now. I trust Him better now. I am grateful for everything He has allotted to me, even that which is perceived as bad by others. No more asking, "Why me?" or "What did I do to deserve this?" Why should I not suffer, when God's perfect Son did? "It pleased the Lord to bruise him," Isaiah said [Isaiah 53:10]. And it pleases the Lord to bruise me. Trials invite us to progress. We all suffer. Great lessons will be learned in our suffering, if we turn to Him. Everything I experience will help me to become more fit for His kingdom, if I submit gratefully to His will.[3]

Disordered patterns of thinking and other physiological and spiritual consequences of living in a fallen world afflict many lives. The lives of King David, Job, Hannah, President George Albert Smith, Martin Luther, Emily Dickinson, Steve Young, George H. Brimhall, Robert L. Millet, Kaye Judd, and the anonymous contributors have much to teach us. Each of these individuals was blessed by God in various ways, even though the degree to which He was intimately involved may not have always been apparent. "The Lord is good to all: and his tender mercies are over all" (Ps. 145:9).

Many of the individuals and families with whom I have worked over the years have overcome mental and emotional adversity and affliction, and have found peace and happiness. Others have not. The mental health problems some people experience may not be resolved until the next life, but most can be managed and even healed in this life if the proper course is taken. I believe, and have observed, that a supportive family, caring leaders, good friends, skilled physicians, modern medicine, competent counselors, and hard work by the individuals involved all play major roles in the healing process. Above all else, the most important factors in overcoming emotional afflictions and mental disorders are discovering, renewing, and maintaining a meaningful relationship with God, following

His guidance, and receiving the redemptive and enabling blessings of the Atonement of Jesus Christ. I pray that each of us will one day return to our Father in Heaven having received the grace of Christ and acquired the lessons of life that will enable us to become as He is.

FURTHER READING

General Resources

Family Services of The Church of Jesus Christ of Latter-day Saints. https://providentliving.churchofjesuschrist.org/lds-family-services?lang=eng.

Firestone, Lisa. "The Importance of the Relationship in Therapy." Psychology Today, December 22, 2016. https://www.psychologytoday.com/us/blog/compassion-matters/201612/the-importance-the-relationship-in-therapy.

General Handbook: Serving in The Church of Jesus Christ of Latter-day Saints. Salt Lake City: The Church of Jesus Christ of Latter-day Saints, 2021. Sections 38.7.7; 38.7.10. https://www.churchofjesuschrist.org/study/manual/general-handbook/38-church-policies-and-guidelines?lang=eng#title_number119.

"Mental Health." The Church of Jesus Christ of Latter-day Saints. https://www.churchofjesuschrist.org/get-help/mental-health. General website for mental health/illness.

National Institute on Mental Health (NIMH). https://www.nimh.nih.gov/. Provides information about mental and emotional disorders and treatments.

"Psychotherapy Works." American Psychological Association. https://www.apa.org/helpcenter/understanding-psychotherapy.

Spiritual and Religious Oriented Psychotherapy project. https://bridgescapstoneconference.wordpress.com/.

"Taking the First Step." National Institute of Mental Health.

https://www.nimh.nih.gov/health/topics/psychotherapies/index.shtml#part_153564.

Transforming the Understanding and Treatment of Mental Illnesses. National Institute of Mental Health, 2019. https://www.nimh.nih.gov/health/statistics/index.shtml.

Depression and Anxiety

"Anxiety Treatments: Know Your Options." Anxiety.org. https://www.anxiety.org/treatments#therapy.

Canadian Mental Health Association. "What's the Difference between Anxiety and an Anxiety Disorder?" HeretoHelp. https://www.heretohelp.bc.ca/q-and-a/whats-the-difference-between-anxiety-and-an-anxiety-disorder.

"Choosing a Therapist." Anxiety and Depression Association of America. https://adaa.org/finding-help/treatment/choosing-therapist.

"How Do I Choose Between Medication and Therapy?" American Psychological Association. https://www.apa.org/ptsd-guideline/patients-and-families/medication-or-therapy.

"Mental Health Medications." National Institutes of Mental Health. https://www.nimh.nih.gov/health/topics/mental-health-medications/index.shtml.

Perfectionism

"Anxiety after My Mission." (video). The Church of Jesus Christ of Latter-day Saints. https://www.churchofjesuschrist.org/inspiration/latter-day-saints-channel/watch/series/his-grace/anxiety-after-my-mission?lang=eng.

"Perfectionism: Will I Ever Be Good Enough?" (video). The Church of Jesus Christ of Latter-day Saints, https://www.churchofjesuschrist.org/inspiration/latter-day-saints-channel/watch/series/his-grace/perfectionism-will-i-ever-be-good-enough?lang=eng.

FURTHER READING

Suicide

"Suicide in America: Frequently Asked Questions." National Institute of Mental Health. https://www.nimh.nih.gov/health/publications/suicide-faq/index.shtml.

Suicide." Gospel Topics. The Church of Jesus Christ of Latter-day Saints. https://www.churchofjesuschrist.org/study/manual/gospel-topics/suicide?lang=eng.

National Suicide Prevention Lifeline. https://suicideprevention lifeline.org/. 1-800-273-8255. In July 2022, the phone number will be 988.

Recommended Books

Frankl, Viktor E. *Man's Search for Meaning*. Boston: Beacon Press, 2006.

Hafen, Bruce C. *The Broken Heart: Applying the Atonement to Life's Experiences*. Salt Lake City: Deseret Book, 2011.

Holland, Jeffrey R. Holland. *Broken Things to Mend*. Salt Lake City: Deseret Book, 2008.

Johnson, Jane Clayson. *Silent Souls Weeping: Depression—Sharing Stories, Finding Hope*. Salt Lake City: Deseret Book, 2019.

Judd, Daniel K. *The Fortunate Fall: Understanding the Blessings and Burdens of Adversity*. Salt Lake City: Deseret Book, 1989.

Robinson, Stephen R. *Believing Christ*. Salt Lake City: Deseret Book, 1992.

Morrison, Alexander B. *Valley of Sorrow: A Layman's Guide to Understanding Mental Illness*. Salt Lake City: Deseret Book, 2003.

Warner, C. Terry. *Bonds That Make Us Free: Healing Our Relationships, Coming to Ourselves*. Salt Lake City: Shadow Mountain, 2001, 23–24.

Williams, Marleen, Dean Belnap, and John Livingstone. *Matters of the Mind: Latter-day Saint Helps for Mental Health*. Salt Lake City: Deseret Book, 2008, 196–219.

Yancey, Phillip. *Where Is God When It Hurts?* Grand Rapids, MI: Zondervan, 1970.

NOTES

Introduction

1. "Depression and Other Common Mental Disorders: Global Health Estimates," World Health Organization, 2017, 5–8, https://www.who.int/publications/i/item/depression-global-health-estimates.
2. "WISQARS—Web-Based Injury Statistics Query and Reporting System," Injury Center, Centers for Disease Control and Prevention (CDC), last reviewed July 1, 2020, https://www.cdc.gov/injury/wisqars/index.html; Opioid Overdose, CDC, last reviewed December 17, 2020, https://www.cdc.gov/drugoverdose/.
3. See Harold G. Koenig, Dana E. King, and Verna Benner Carson, *Handbook of Religion and Health*, 2nd ed. (Oxford: Oxford University Press, 2012).
4. J. D. Bartz, P. S. Richards, T. B. Smith, and L. Fischer, "A 17-Year Longitudinal Study of Religion and Mental Health in a Mormon Sample," *Mental Health, Religion and Culture* 13, no. 7 (2010): 683–95; see also L. C. Jensen, J. Jensen, and T. Wiederhold, "Religiosity, Denomination, and Mental Health among Young Men and Women, *Psychological Reports* (1993): 72, 1157–58.
5. Adapted from "Transforming the Understanding and Treatment of Mental Illnesses," National Institute of Mental Health, 2019, https://www.nimh.nih.gov/health/statistics/index.shtml.
6. See Daniel K Judd, *Religion, Mental Health, and the Latter-day Saints*, (Provo, UT: Brigham Young University, Religious Studies Center, 1999); see also Jared L. Overton, "Latter-day Saints and Mental Health: A Review of the Literature, 1995–2005" (PhD diss., Azusa Pacific University, October 2005).
7. "Seeking Information from Reliable Sources," *General Handbook: Serving in The Church of Jesus Christ of Latter-day Saints* (Salt Lake City: The Church of Jesus Christ of Latter-day Saints, 2021), 38.8.45, https://www.churchofjesuschrist.org/study/manual/general-handbook/38-church-policies-and-guidelines?lang=eng#title_number2.
8. Many of the research studies cited in this publication are correlational and not causal. When two realities appear to be related, one does not necessarily cause the other. This concern is commonly known as "the fallacy of false cause." See S. Morris Engel, *With Good Reason:*

An Introduction to Informal Fallacies (New York: St. Martin's Press, 1990), 153–59.

9. See Daniel K Judd, *The Fortunate Fall: Understanding the Blessings and Burdens of Adversity* (Salt Lake City: Deseret Book, 2011).
10. Russell M. Nelson, "There Is No Conflict between Science and Religion," Church News, April 17, 2015, https://www.thechurchnews.com/archives/2015-04-14/elder-nelson-dedicates-life-sciences-building-there-is-no-conflict-between-science-and-religion-34270.
11. Russell M. Nelson, "Revelation for the Church, Revelations for Our Lives," *Ensign*, May 2018, 94–95.
12. C. S. Lewis, *Mere Christianity* (New York: Collier Books, 1960), 86.
13. Ezra Taft Benson, "A Witness and a Warning," *Ensign*, November 1979, 31.
14. "*Times and Seasons*, 15 June 1842," 823, The Joseph Smith Papers, accessed January 6, 2020, https://www.josephsmithpapers.org/paper-summary/times-and-seasons-15-june-1842/9.
15. Boyd K. Packer, "Covenants," *Ensign*, November 1990, 85.
16. "Letter to Israel Daniel Rupp, 5 June 1844," [1], The Joseph Smith Papers, https://www.josephsmithpapers.org/paper-summary/letter-to-israel-daniel-rupp-5-june-1844/1. Spelling standardized.
17. See Alvin Plantinga, "Reason and Belief in God," in *Faith and Rationality: Reasons and Belief in God*, ed. Alvin Plantinga and Nicholas Wolterstorff (Notre Dame, IN: University of Notre Dame Press, 1984), 87.
18. David A. Bednar, "We Will Prove Them Herewith," *Ensign*, November 2020, 11.
19. Richard N. Williams and Edwin E. Gantt, "Introduction: Science, Scientism, and Psychology," in *On Hijacking Science: Exploring the Nature and Consequences of Overreach in Psychology*, ed. Edwin E. Gantt and Richard N. Williams (New York: Routledge, 2018), 9.
20. Bertrand Russell, *Science and Religion*, rev. 2nd ed (Oxford: Oxford University Press, 1997), 243.
21. Joseph F. Smith, in *Juvenile Instructor*, September 1902, 562.

Chapter 1: Depression, Sickness, Sorrow, and the Gospel of Jesus Christ

1. Jeffrey R. Holland, "Like a Broken Vessel," *Ensign*, November 2013, 40.
2. See "Depressive Disorders," in *Diagnostic and Statistical Manual of Mental Disorders*, 5th ed. (Washington, DC: American Psychiatric Association, 2013), 161. Hereafter cited as DSM-5.
3. As cited in Mary Jane Woodger, "'Cheat the Asylum of a Victim': George Albert Smith's 1909–12 Breakdown," *Journal of Mormon History* 34, no. 4 (Fall 2008): 116.
4. Heber J. Sears to George Albert Smith, April 12, 1909, George A. Smith Papers, MS 36, box 32, folder 11, Special Collections, Marriott

NOTES

Library, University of Utah, Salt Lake City. Spelling and punctuation standardized.

5. Robert Bartholow, "What Is Meant by Nervous Prostration?" *The Boston Medical and Surgical Journal* CX, no. 3 (1884): 53.
6. John Henry Smith to George Albert Smith, April 9, 1909, George A. Smith Papers, box 29, folder 6. Special Collections, Marriott Library.
7. See David Scott-Macnab, "The Many Faces of the Noonday Demon," *Journal of Early Christian History* 8, no. 1 (2018): 22–42.
8. George Albert Smith to Ralph E. Woolley February 6, 1937, George A. Smith Papers, box 69, folder 19, Special Collections, Marriott Library.
9. George Albert Smith, as cited in Mary Jane Woodger, *Against the Odds: The Life of George Albert Smith, His Creed and Teachings* (American Fork, UT: Covenant Communications, 2011).
10. Allen Frances, *Saving Normal* (New York: William Morrow, 2014), 155.
11. Allan V. Horwitz and Jerome C. Wakefield, *The Loss of Sadness: How Psychiatry Transformed Normal Sorrow into Depressive Disorder* (New York: Oxford University Press, 2007), 6.
12. *APA Dictionary of Psychology*, 2nd ed. (Washington, DC: American Psychological Association, 2015), loc. 24000–24001, Kindle.
13. *APA Dictionary of Psychology*, loc. 49529–49530.
14. *APA Dictionary of Psychology*, loc. 45673–45674.
15. Russell M. Nelson, "Joy and Spiritual Survival," *Ensign* November 2016, 82.
16. A. M. Leventhal, "Sadness, Depression, and Avoidance Behavior," *Behavior Modification* 32, no. 6 (2008): 759.
17. DSM-5, 161.
18. Adapted from Liubov Ben-Noun, "Mental Disorder That Afflicted King David the Great," *History of Psychiatry* 15 (2004): 467–76.
19. D. M. Howard Jr., in *The Anchor Yale Bible Dictionary*, vol. 2, ed D. N. Freedman (New York: Doubleday, 1992), 41.
20. Boyd K. Packer, "The Touch of the Master's Hand," *Ensign*, May 2001, 22–24.
21. Albert Ellis, "There Is No Place for the Concept of Sin in Psychotherapy," *Journal of Counseling Psychology 7*, no. 3 (1960); 189; emphasis added.
22. Jay E. Adams, *Competent to Counsel: An Introduction to Nouthetic Counseling* (Grand Rapids, MI: Zondervan, 1970), 17; emphasis added.
23. Holland, "Like a Broken Vessel," *Ensign* November 2013, 40.
24. Jeffrey R. Holland, *However Long and Hard the Road* (Salt Lake City: Deseret Book, 1985), 6.
25. Boyd K. Packer, "The Brilliant Morning of Forgiveness," *Ensign*, November 1995, 19–20.
26. James E. Faust, "The Great Imitator," *Ensign*, November 1987, 35.

NOTES

27. Barbara Brown Taylor, *Leaving Church: A Memoir of Faith* (New York: HarperOne, 2012), 106.
28. Dieter F. Uchtdorf, "The Merciful Obtain Mercy," *Ensign*, May 2012, 75.
29. Henry B. Eyring, "Spiritual Preparedness: Start Early and Be Steady," *Ensign*, November 2005, 37.
30. Boyd K. Packer, "Why Stay Morally Clean," *Ensign*, July 1972.
31. Jane Clayson Johnson, *Silent Souls Weeping: Depression—Sharing Stories Finding Hope* (Salt Lake City: Deseret Book, 2019), 163.
32. S. R. Forkus, N. H. Weiss, A. A. Contractor, J. G. Breines, and P. Dranger, "PTSD's Blame Criterion and Mental Health Outcomes in a Community Mental Health Treatment-Seeking Sample," *Psychological Trauma: Theory, Research, Practice, and Policy* 12, no. 1 (2020): 30.
33. See M. L. Fisher and J. J. Exline, "Moving Toward Self-Forgiveness: Removing Barriers Related to Shame, Guilt, and Regret," *Social and Personality Psychology Compass* 4, no. 8 (2010): 548. See also D&C 64:8–12.
34. John Gottman and Julie Gottman, "The Natural Principles of Love," *Journal of Family Theory and Review* 9, no. 1 (2017): 13; see also Kyle Benson, "The Magic Relationship Ratio, According to Science," The Gottman Institute, October 4, 2017, https://www.gottman.com/blog/the-magic-relationship-ratio-according-science/.
35. Jack Zenger and Joseph Folkman, "The Ideal Praise-to-Criticism Ratio," *Harvard Business Review*, March 15, 2013, https://hbr.org/2013/03/the-ideal-praise-to-criticism.
36. DSM-5, 160.
37. T. M. Cousineau and A. D. Domar, "Psychological Impact of Infertility, *Best Practice and Research: Clinical Obstetrics and Gynecology* 21, no. 2 (April 2007): 293–94.
38. Boyd K. Packer, "Solving Emotional Problems in the Lord's Own Way," *Ensign*, January 2010, 50–51.

Chapter 2: Anxiety and the Grace of Jesus Christ

1. B. Bandelow and S. Michaelis, "Epidemiology of Anxiety Disorders in the 21st Century," *Dialogues in Clinical Neuroscience* 17, no. 3 (2015): 331.
2. "Any Anxiety Disorder," National Institute of Mental Health, last updated November 2017, https://www.nimh.nih.gov/health/statistics/any-anxiety-disorder.shtml.
3. K. S. Kendler, review of *The Loss of Sadness: How Psychiatry Transformed Normal Sorrow into Depressive Disorder*, by Allan V Horwitz and Jerome C. Wakefield, *Psychological Medicine* 38, no. 1 (2008): 148–50.
4. DSM-5, 189.
5. J. Strack, P. Lopes, F. Esteves, and P. Fernandez-Berrocal, "Must We Suffer to Succeed?: When Anxiety Boosts Motivation and

NOTES

     Performance," *Journal of Individual Differences* 38, no. 2 (2017): 113–24.
6. As cited in Alan V. Horwitz and Jerome C. Wakefield, *All We Have to Fear: Psychiatry's Transformation of Natural Anxieties into Mental Disorders* (New York: Oxford University Press, 2012), 5.
7. "Anxiety Treatments: Know Your Options," Anxiety.org, accessed September 3, 2020, https://www.anxiety.org/treatments#therapy.
8. Adapted from the Canadian Mental Health Association, "What's the Difference between Anxiety and an Anxiety Disorder?" HeretoHelp, 2015, https://www.heretohelp.bc.ca/q-and-a/whats-the-difference-between-anxiety-and-an-anxiety-disorder.
9. Personal correspondence with the author. Used with permission.
10. C. H. Miller and D. H. Hedges, "Scrupulosity Disorder: An Overview and Introductory Analysis," *Journal of Anxiety Disorders* 22 (2008): 1042–58.
11. Personal correspondence with the author; emphasis added. Used with permission.
12. *Luther's Works*, ed. Jaroslav Pelikan (St. Louis: Concordia Publishing House, 1955), 27:13.
13. M. Russell Ballard, "Building Bridges of Understanding," *Ensign*, June 1998, 65.
14. As cited in Roland C. Bainton, *Here I Stand: A Life of Martin Luther* (Peabody, MA: Hendrikson Publishers, 1950, repr. 2012), 26.
15. Russell M. Nelson, "Closing Remarks," *Ensign*, November 2019, 121.
16. *Luther's Works*, 27:13.
17. James Kittelson, *Luther the Reformer* (Minneapolis: Augsburg Fortress Publishing, 1986), 79.
18. *Luther's Works*, 5:157.
19. Bainton, *Here I Stand*, 35.
20. See G. Fond, A. Macgregor, M. Leboyer, and A. Michalsen, "Fasting in Mood Disorders: Neurobiology and Effectiveness. A Review of the Literature," *Psychiatry Research* 209, no. 3 (October 30, 2013): 253.
21. *Luther's Works*, 54:339.
22. *Luther's Works*, 44:74–75.
23. *Luther's Works*, 54:340.
24. *Luther's Works*, 54:85.
25. Jeffrey R. Holland, "Be Ye Therefore Perfect—Eventually," *Ensign*, November 2017, 41; emphasis in original. See also "Perfectionism: Will I Ever Be Good Enough?" (video), The Church of Jesus Christ of Latter-day Saints, accessed April 20, 2020, https://www.churchofjesuschrist.org/inspiration/latter-day-saints-channel/watch/series/his-grace/perfectionism-will-i-ever-be-good-enough?lang=eng.
26. Richard Marius, *Martin Luther: The Christian between God and Death* (Cambridge: Harvard University Press, 1999), 212–13.
27. *Luther's Works*, 34:336–37.
28. *Luther's Works*, 54:193–94.

29. Dieter F. Uchtdorf, "The Gift of Grace," *Ensign*, May 2015, 109; emphasis added.
30. See "Anxiety after My Mission" (video), The Church of Jesus Christ of Latter-day Saints, accessed April 20, 2020, https://www.churchofjesuschrist.org/inspiration/latter-day-saints-channel/watch/series/his-grace/anxiety-after-my-mission?lang=eng.
31. Dietrich Bonhoeffer, *The Cost of Discipleship* (New York: Touchstone, 1995), 44–45, emphasis in original.
32. Robert L. Millet, *After All We Can Do . . . Grace Works* (Salt Lake City: Deseret Book, 2003), 144. See also 2 Ne. 25:23; Mosiah 2:21–22.
33. Daniel K Judd, W. Justin Dyer, and Justin B. Top, "Grace, Legalism, and Mental Health: Examining Direct and Mediating Relationships," *Journal of the Psychology of Religion and Spirituality* 12, no. 1 (2020): 26–35.
34. M. Russell Ballard, "Building Bridges of Understanding," *Ensign*, June 1998, 65.
35. The DSM-5 no longer includes obsessive-compulsive disorder, post-traumatic stress disorder, and acute stress disorder as anxiety disorders; they are now classified separately.
36. DSM-5.
37. See Marryanne M. Garbowsky, *The House without the Door: A Study of Emily Dickinson and the Illness of Agoraphobia* (Madison, NJ: Farleigh Dickinson University Press, 1989), 21.
38. See T. J. Barloon and R. Noyes, "Charles Darwin and Panic Disorder, *Journal of the American Medical Association* (1997): 277, 138–41.
39. See Helen Saul, *Phobias: Fighting the Fear* (New York: Arcade Publishing, 2001), 6.
40. Steve Young, *QB: My Life behind the Spiral* (Boston: Houghton Mifflin Harcourt, 2016), 124.
41. Young, *QB: My Life behind the Spiral*, 246.
42. Steve Young, interview, September 20, 2017. Transcript in the possession of the author. Used with permission.

Chapter 3: Psychotic Disorders, Self-Deception, and Personal Revelation

1. Isaac Woodbridge Riley, *The Founder of Mormonism: A Psychological Study of Joseph Smith*, Jr. (London: William Heinemann, 1903), 70.
2. A. Ellis, "Psychotherapy and Atheistic Values: A Response to A. E. Bergin's 'Psychotherapy and Religious Values,'" *Journal of Consulting and Clinical Psychology* 48, no. 5 (1980): 635–39.
3. H. D. Delaney, W. R. Miller, and A. M. Bisonó, "Religiosity and Spirituality among Psychologists: A Survey of Clinician Members of the American Psychological Association," *Spirituality in Clinical Practice* 1, S (2013): 95–106.
4. Bernard Spilka and Kevin L. Ladd, *The Psychology of Prayer: A*

NOTES

Scientific Approach (New York: Guilford Publications, 2012), 3. The research was drawn from the 2008 General Social Survey.

5. "Growing Share of Americans Say They Seldom or Never Pray," Pew Research Center, October 29, 2015, https://www.pewforum.org/2015/11/03/u-s-public-becoming-less-religious/pf-2015-11-03_rls_ii-45/.

6. "History, 1838–1856, volume C-1 [2 November 1838–31 July 1842]," 1305, The Joseph Smith Papers, accessed December 6, 2020, https://www.josephsmithpapers.org/paper-summary/history-1838-1856-volume-c-1-2-november-1838-31-july-1842/479.

7. P. Rudalevičiene, T. Stompe, A. Narbekovas, N. Raŝkauskiene, and R. Bunevičius, "Are Religious Delusions Related to Religiosity in Schizophrenia?" *Medicina* 44, no. 7 (2008): 529–35. Percentages of religious content vary from country and culture.

8. "History, 1838–1856, volume E-1 [1 July 1843–30 April 1844]," 1974, The Joseph Smith Papers, accessed March 4, 2020, https://www.josephsmithpapers.org/paper-summary/history-1838-1856-volume-e-1-1-july-1843-30-april-1844/346.

9. C. Terry Warner, *Bonds That Make Us Free: Healing Our Relationships, Coming to Ourselves* (Salt Lake City: Shadow Mountain, 2001), 23–24.

10. See Lisa Feldman Barrett, *How Emotions Are Made: The Secret Life of the Brain* (Boston: Mariner Books, 2017), 25–41. See also Daniel K Judd, Ronald D. Bingham, and Richard N. Williams, "Agentive Theory as Therapy: An Outcome Study," *Issues in Religion and Psychotherapy* 14, no. 1 (1988), article 5.

11. Personal correspondence with the author, July 5, 2020. Used with permission.

12. Merriam-Webster, s.v. "schizophrenia," accessed February 25, 2020, https://www.merriam-webster.com/dictionary/schizophrenia.

13. Thomas McGlashan, "Natural History of Schizophrenia," *Schizophrenia Bulletin* 14, no. 4 (1988): 528.

14. Personal correspondence with the author, March 16, 2020. Used with permission.

15. Personal correspondence with the author, March 16, 2020. Used with permission.

16. For a detailed account of a young man's experience with schizophrenia, see A. Reina, "The Spectrum of Sanity and Insanity," *Schizophrenia Bulletin* 36, no. 1 (2010): 3–8.

17. See Daniel K Judd, *The Fortunate Fall: Understanding the Blessings and Burdens of Adversity* (Salt Lake City: Deseret Book, 2011).

Chapter 4: Parents, Children, and Mental Health

1. C. Broderick, *My Parents Married on a Dare and Other Favorite Essays on Life* (Salt Lake City: Deseret Book, 1996), 87–89.

2. R. J. Matthews, *A Bible! A Bible!* (Salt Lake City: Bookcraft, 1990), 272.

3. See F. Nunes and C. P. Mota, "Parenting Styles and Suicidal Ideation in Adolescents: Mediating Effect of Attachment," *Journal of Child and Family Studies* 26, no. 3 (2017): 745.
4. Dallin H. Oaks, "Love and Law," *Ensign*, November 2009, 28; emphasis added.
5. Nunes and Mota, "Parenting Styles and Suicidal Ideation in Adolescents, 745. See also Keith A. King, Rebecca A. Vidourek, and Ashley L. Merianos, "Authoritarian Parenting and Youth Depression: Results from a National Study," *Journal of Prevention & Intervention in the Community* 44, no. 2 (2016): 130–39.
6. See W. J. Dyer, M. A. Goodman, and S. A. Hardy, "Adolescent Suicide Ideation in Utah: The Role of Religion and Family," *Psychology of Religion and Spirituality*, 2020, https://doi.org/10.1037/rel0000319.
7. C. H. Hart, L. D. Newell, and J. H. Haupt, "Parenting with Love, Limits, and Latitude: Proclamation Principles and Supportive Scholarship," in *Successful Marriages and Families: Proclamation Principles and Research Perspectives*, ed. A. J. Hawkins, D. C. Dollahite, and T. D. Draper (Provo, UT: BYU Press, 2012), 104–17.
8. "Leading Causes of Death and Injury," Centers for Disease Control and Prevention, last updated February 9, 2021, https://www.cdc.gov/injury/wisqars/leadingcauses.html.
9. "Fatal Injury Mapping," Centers for Disease Control and Prevention, last updated August 7, 2013, https://wisqars.cdc.gov:8443/cdcMapFramework/mapModuleInterface.jsp.
10. Francis Annor, Amanda Wilkinson, and Marissa Zwalk, "Epi-Aid # 2017–019: Undetermined Risk Factors for Suicide among Youth Aged 10–17 Years—Utah, 2017: Final Report," Utah Department of Health, November 2017, 46, http://health.utah.gov/vipp/pdf/Suicide/CDCEpi-AidReport.pdf. See also Sterling C. Hilton, Gilbert W. Fellingham, and Joseph L. Lyon, "Suicide Rates and Religious Commitment in Young Adult Males in Utah," *American Journal of Epidemiology* 155 (2002): 415.
11. The Reconciliation and Growth Project is a group of mental health professionals whose goal is "fostering dialogue among people with differing perspectives on faith-based values and sexual and gender diversity. See https://reconciliationandgrowth.org/.
12. Stephen Cranney, "The LGB Mormon Paradox: Mental, Physical, and Self-Rated Health among Mormon and Non-Mormon LGB Individuals in the Utah Behavioral Risk Factor Surveillance System," *Journal of Homosexuality* 64, no. 6 (2017): 731–44.
13. M. Russell Ballard, "Questions and Answers" (BYU Devotional, November 14, 2017), https://speeches.byu.edu/talks/m-russell-ballard/questions-and-answers/.
14. "Suicide in America: Frequently Asked Questions," National Institute of Mental Health, accessed April 6, 2020, https://www.nimh.nih.gov/health/publications/suicide-faq/index.shtml.
15. "Suicide," Gospel Topics, The Church of Jesus Christ of Latter-day

Saints, accessed April 6, 2020, https://www.churchofjesuschrist.org/study/manual/gospel-topics/suicide?lang=eng. Includes religious resources.
16. A. Richard Rice, *God's Foreknowledge and Man's Free Will* (Minneapolis: Bethany House, 1985), 10.
17. "History, 1838–1856, volume E-1 [1 July 1843–30 April 1844]," 1968–70, The Joseph Smith Papers, accessed March 1, 2018, http://www.josephsmithpapers.org/paper-summary/history-1838-1856-volume-e-1-1-july-1843-30-april-1844/340.
18. Heber C. Kimball, in *Journal of Discourses*, 4:222 (February 8, 1857).
19. Richard Dawkins, *The God Delusion* (Boston: Mariner Books, 2008), 51.
20. Jeffrey R. Holland, "The Grandeur of God," *Ensign*, November 2003, 73.
21. Dallin H. Oaks, "Powerful Ideas," *Ensign*, November 1995, 25.
22. W. W. Phelps, "The Answer," letter to William Smith, December 25, 1844, *Times and Seasons* 5, no. 24 (1844): 758. See also Jer. 44:17.
23. Erastus Snow, in *Journal of Discourses*, 19:270 (March 3, 1878).
24. President Hinckley taught: "It has been said that the Prophet Joseph Smith made no correction to what Sister Snow had written. Therefore, we have a Mother in Heaven. Therefore [some assume] that we may appropriately pray to her. Logic and reason would certainly suggest that if we have a Father in Heaven, we have a Mother in Heaven. That doctrine rests well with me. However, in light of what we have received from the Lord Himself, I regard it as inappropriate for anyone in the Church to pray to our Mother in Heaven." *Teachings of Gordon B. Hinckley* (Salt Lake City: Deseret Book, 1997), 56–57.
25. H. T. G. Chou and D. Uata, "The Impact of Parental Discipline on the Image of God," *Mental Health, Religion and Culture* 15, no. 7 (2012): 677–88.
26. Karen Armstrong, *A History of God* (New York: Ballantine Books, 1993), 357.
27. K. I. Pargament, "The Bitter and the Sweet: An Evaluation of the Costs and Benefits of Religiousness," *Psychological Inquiry* 13, no. 3 (2002): 168–81.
28. Maurice S. Murunga, Alicia Limke-McLean, and Ronald W. Wright, "Who's Your Daddy? Family Structure Differences in Attachment to God," *Journal of Psychology and Theology* 45, no. 3 (2017): 205.
29. This chapter was adapted from an address given by the author at the Reason for Hope conference at Brigham Young University on April 6, 2018.

Chapter 5: Healing the Broken Brain

1. "Dr. George H. Brimhall Meets Death at Home," *Provo (UT) Evening Sunday Herald* 9, no. 50 (July 31, 1932): 1.
2. George Albert Smith, funeral address, as cited in Mary Jane Woodger and Joseph H. Groberg, *From the Muddy River to the Ivory Tower: The*

Journey of George H. Brimhall (Provo, UT: Brigham Young University Press, 2010), 206.
3. Thomas S. Monson to Daniel K Judd, November 4. 2013. Private correspondence in possession of the author.
4. M. Russell Ballard, "Suicide: Some Things We Know, and Some We Do Not," *Ensign*, October 1987.
5. Neal A. Maxwell, "According to the Desire of Our Hearts," *Ensign*, November 1996, 21.
6. Dallin H. Oaks, "Free Agency and Freedom," in *The Book of Mormon: Second Nephi, the Doctrinal Structure*, ed. M. Nyman and C. Tate (Salt Lake City: Bookcraft, 1989), 10.
7. "Traumatic Brain Injury," Mayo Clinic, accessed May 1, 2020, https://www.mayoclinic.org/diseases-conditions/traumatic-brain-injury/symptoms-causes/syc-20378557.
8. *"Pass It On": The Story of Bill Wilson and How the A. A. Message Reached the World* (New York: World Services, 1984), 252, 258n.
9. Daniel K Judd, "Moral Agency: A Doctrinal Application to Therapy," *Issues in Religion and Psychotherapy* 24, no. 1 (1999), http://scholarsarchive.byu.edu/irp/vol24/iss1/11.
10. Attributed to Napoleon Hill, *Think and Grow Rich* (The Ralston Society, 1937).
11. P. Scott Richards and Allen E. Bergin, *A Spiritual Strategy for Counseling and Psychotherapy*, 2nd ed. (Washington, DC: American Psychological Association, 2005), 103–4.
12. See Charles W. Elliot, ed., *The Apology, Phaedo and Crito of Plato; Golden Sayings of Epictetus; Meditations of Marcus Aurelius: Part 2*, Harvard Classics (Whitefish, MT: Kessinger Publishing Company, 2004), 55.
13. Roger E. Olson, *The Story of Christian Theology: Twenty Centuries of Tradition and Reform* (Downers Grove, IL: InterVarsity Press, 1999), 322.
14. Dallin H. Oaks, "Apostasy and Restoration," *Ensign*, May 1995.
15. Russell M. Nelson, "Hear Him," *Ensign*, May 2020, https://www.churchofjesuschrist.org/study/general-conference/2020/04/45nelson?lang=eng.
16. See Anne Harrington, *Mind Fixers: Psychiatry's Troubled Search for the Biology of Mental Illness* (New York: W. W. Norton, 2019).
17. See Peter D. Kramer, *Ordinarily Well: The Case for Anti-Depressants* (New York: Farrar, Straus, and Giroux, 2016), 3.
18. See David Mischoulon and Jerrold F. Rosenbaum, eds., *Natural Medications for Psychiatric Disorders: Considering the Alternatives*, 2nd ed. (Philadelphia: Lippincott, Williams & Wilkins, 2008). See also N. Lee Smith, "Herbal Remedies: God's Medicine?" *Dialogue: A Journal of Mormon Thought* 12, no. 3 (1979): 37–60.
19. Hugh B. Brown, "They Call for New Light," *The Improvement Era* 67, no. 6 (1964): 458.

NOTES

20. David A. Bednar, "In the Strength of the Lord" (BYU Devotional, Provo, UT, October 23, 2001); emphasis added.
21. Dallin H. Oaks, "Strengthened by the Atonement of Jesus Christ," *Ensign*, November 2015.
22. Jeffrey R. Holland, "Like a Broken Vessel," *Ensign*, November 2013.
23. "How Do I Choose Between Medication and Therapy?" American Psychological Association, accessed on April 29, 2020, https://www.apa.org/ptsd-guideline/patients-and-families/medication-or-therapy.
24. Alexander B. Morrison, *Valley of Sorrow: A Layman's Guide to Understanding Mental Illness* (Salt Lake City: Deseret Book, 2003), xv.
25. Gerald Corey, *Theory and Practice of Counseling and Psychotherapy*, 10th ed. (Boston: Cengage Learning, 2016), 450.
26. "Taking the First Step," National Institute of Mental Health, accessed April 29, 2020, https://www.nimh.nih.gov/health/topics/psychotherapies/index.shtml#part_153564.
27. Richard L. Evans (address to the young people at the Northwest Inland Division gathered for Zion's Camp, October 15, 1971), as cited in David A. Bednar, "Your Whole Soul as an Offering unto Him" (Rick's College Devotional, Rexburg, ID, January 5, 1999); emphasis added.
28. C. Stamoulos, L. Trepanier, S. Bourkas, S. Bradley, K. Stelmaszczyk, D. Schwartzman, and M. Drapeau, "Psychologists' Perceptions of the Importance of Common Factors in Psychotherapy for Successful Treatment Outcomes," *Journal of Psychotherapy Integration* 26, no. 3 (2016): 300–317. See also Lisa Firestone, "The Importance of the Relationship in Therapy," *Psychology Today*, December 22, 2016, https://www.psychologytoday.com/us/blog/compassion-matters/201612/the-importance-the-relationship-in-therapy.
29. See "Counseling Services," Family Services, The Church of Jesus Christ of Latter-day Saints, accessed February 7, 2021, https://providentliving.churchofjesuschrist.org/lds-family-services/counseling-services?lang=eng.
30. "Choosing a Therapist," Anxiety and Depression Association of America, accessed May 2, 2020, https://adaa.org/finding-help/treatment/choosing-therapist.
31. See K. M. Benes, J. M. Walsh, M. R. McMinn, A. W. Dominguez, and D. C. Aikins, "Psychology and the Church: An Exemplar of Psychologist–Clergy Collaboration, *Professional Psychology: Research and Practice* 31, no. 5 (2000).
32. Kenneth S. Kendler, "Toward a Philosophical Structure of Psychiatry," *American Journal of Psychiatry* 162 (2005): 433–40. Even though many different perspectives have been shared over the years by the popular media, academic journals, mental health professionals, family physicians, and religious leaders, the explanation that mental illness is caused by "chemical imbalances" isn't generally supported by clinical research.

NOTES

33. Morrison, *Valley of Sorrow*, 56.
34. Kendler, "Toward a Philosophical Structure of Psychiatry," 433–40.
35. "Mental Health Medications," National Institutes of Mental Health, accessed April 29, 2020, https://www.nimh.nih.gov/health/topics/mental-health-medications/index.shtml.
36. Adapted from Corey, *Theory and Practice of Counseling and Psychotherapy*, 438.
37. Hugh B. Brown, "They Call For New Light," *The Improvement Era*, June 1964, 458; from a general conference address given on April 5, 1964.
38. Dallin H. Oaks, "Racism and Other Challenges" (BYU Devotional, Provo, UT, October 27, 2020).

Chapter 6: Healing the Broken Heart

1. *Teachings of Gordon B. Hinckley* (Salt Lake City: The Church of Jesus Christ of Latter-day Saints, 1997), 648.
2. See Spiritual and Religious Oriented Psychotherapy Project, accessed: September 10, 2020, https://bridgescapstoneconference.wordpress.com/.
3. P. S. Richards, P. W, Sanders, T. Lea, J. A. McBride, and G. E. K. Allen, "Bringing Spiritually Oriented Psychotherapies into the Health Care Mainstream: A Call for Worldwide Collaboration," *Spirituality in Clinical Practice* 2, no. 3 (2015): 169.
4. Personal correspondence with the author, April 2020. Used with permission.
5. R. S. El-Mallakh, Y. Gao, and R. Jeannie Roberts, "Tardive Dysphoria: The Role of Long Term Antidepressant Use in-Inducing Chronic Depression. *Medical Hypotheses* 76, no. 6 (2011): 769.
6. Personal correspondence with the author, April 2020. Used with permission.
7. Personal correspondence with the author, July 2020. Used with permission.
8. D. Todd Christofferson, "The Power of Covenants," *Ensign*, May 2009, accessed, May 4, 2020, https://www.churchofjesuschrist.org/study/general-conference/2009/04/the-power-of-covenants?lang=eng.
9. Robert L. Millet, *Holding Fast: Dealing with Doubt in the Latter Days* (Salt Lake City: Deseret Book, 2008), 44.
10. Jeffrey R. Holland, "Like a Broken Vessel, *Ensign*, November 2013, 41.
11. Millet, *Holding Fast*, 45.
12. Robert L. Millet, remarks in meeting with seminary and institute personnel, Orem, UT, August 7, 2019. Document in possession of the author.
13. Robert L. Millet to Daniel K Judd, email, May 27, 2020. Used with permission.
14. This particular change in the text is one of the changes that wasn't included in the footnotes or in the appendix of the edition of the

scriptures published by The Church of Jesus Christ of Latter-day Saints. The majority of the changes the Prophet Joseph Smith made are included in the edition of the Bible published by Herald Publishing House. See http://www.centerplace.org/hs/iv/iv-mat.htm.
15. Boyd K. Packer, "Do Not Fear," *Ensign,* May 2004, 77
16. Miriam Greenspan, *Healing Through the Dark Emotions: The Wisdom of Grief, Fear, and Despair* (Boulder: Shambhala, 2003), 7–8.
17. T. E. Joiner Jr., K. A. Van Orden, T. K. Witte, and D. Rudd, *The Interpersonal Theory of Suicide: Guidance for Working with Suicidal Clients* (Washington, DC: American Psychological Association, 2009), 7.
18. S. Stack and J. Scourfield, "Recency of Divorce, Depression, and Suicide Risk," *Journal of Family Issues* 26, no. 6 (2015): 695–715.
19. See "Mental Health" The Church of Jesus Christ of Latter-day Saints, accessed April 7, 2020, https://www.churchofjesuschrist.org/get-help/mental-health. See also "Depression Support and Advocacy," Mental Health America," accessed April 7, 2020, https://www.mhanational.org/depression-support-and-advocacy.
20. See J. Rottenberg, A. R. Devendorf, T. B. Kashdan, and D. J. Disabato, "The Curious Neglect of High Functioning after Psychopathology: The Case of Depression," *Perspectives on Psychological Science* 13, no. 5 (2018): 549–66.
21. Neal A. Maxwell, *"For the Power Is in Them:" Mormon Musings* (Salt Lake City: Deseret Book, 1970), 48–49.
22. Ezra Taft Benson, "Do Not Despair," Ensign, October 1986, 2. Scripture citations added.
23. *The Teachings of Howard W. Hunter* (Salt Lake City: The Church of Jesus Christ of Latter-day Saints, 2015), 40.

Conclusion

1. George H. Brimhall's title at BYU was director of the Department of Theology and Religion. Gary James Bergera and Ronald Priddis, *Brigham Young University: A House of Faith*, (Salt Lake City: Signature Books, 1985), 15.
2. George H. Brimhall, as cited in Woodger and Groberg, *From the Muddy River to the Ivory Tower: The Journey of George H. Brimhall* (Provo, UT: BYU Studies, 2010), 154.
3. Personal communication to the author, July 7, 2020. Used with permission.

INDEX

Abraham, 53
Accountability, 75–79
Adams, Jay E., 23
Adler, Alfred, 89
Adlerian therapy, 89
Adult children, behavior of, 67
Agency: and self-deception, 56–61; and war in heaven, 66–67; and accountability, 77–79
Agoraphobia, 49
Allen, G. E. Kawika, 93
Amulek, 56–57
Antidepressants, 96. *See also* Medication
Anxiety: common, 34–35; treating, 35–36; scrupulosity as, 36–38; of Martin Luther, 38–42; and perfectionism, 42–43; and grace of Christ, 43–48; manifestations of, 48–49; examples of those suffering with, 49–51; and self-deception, 59–60
Atonement, 5–6; healing through, 24–26, 94–98; peace and salvation through, 44; resisting redemptive and enabling powers of, 82
Augustinian monks, 39–40
Authoritarian parenting, 65–68, 69
Authoritative parenting, 68

Ballard, M. Russell, 39, 47, 70, 76
Barrenness, 30–33

Bartholow, Roberts, 15
Basinger, Kim, 49
Bathsheba, 22
Beck, Aaron, 89
Bednar, David A, 10, 82
Behavior therapy, 89
Benson, Ezra Taft, 7–8, 108
Bergin, Allen E., 93
"Bibliotherapy," 101
Bitterness, 28
Blame, for ourselves or others, 26, 27–28, 29
Body, spirit and, 80
Bonhoeffer, Dietrich, 46
Bowen, Murray, 90
Brimhall, George H., 75–76, 81, 110–12
Broderick, Carlfred, 65–66
"Broken vessel," being like, 20–21
Brown, Hugh B., 81, 90–91

Chastity, law of, 67
Cheap grace, 46–47
Cheerfulness, of God, 71
Children, adult, 67. *See also* Parenting
Christofferson, D. Todd, 97–98
Church leaders, counsel of, 87
Church of Jesus Christ of Latter-day Saints, The: and relationship between religious belief and practice and mental health, 3–5; misunderstanding and misapplication of doctrine and principles of, 5

INDEX

Cognitive behavior therapy (CBT), 89–90
Cohabitation, 67
Confession, 41
Correction, constructive, 29–30
Cotton, James, 100–101
Counseling, 82–87, 89–91, 93–94
Counterfeit opposites, 7–11
Covenants, 97–98
Creation, 5–6
Criticism, 27–28, 75–76

Darwin, Charles, 49
David, King, 20–23
Davis, Miles, 35
Dawkins, Richard, 71
Delusions, psychotic, 54–56
Depletion depression, 98–102
Depression: of Jeffrey R. Holland, 12–13; of George Albert Smith, 13–17; dimensions in dealing with, 16; versus sorrow, 17–19, 20; of King David, 20–23; sin and, 23–26; of Job, 26; and criticisms of others, 27–28; enduring, 28–29; and accepting personal responsibility, 29–30; symptoms of, 30–31; of Hannah, 30–33; and self-deception, 59–60; of George H. Brimhall, 75; cause and treatment of, 87–88; and feeling Spirit, 94–96; of Robert L. Millet, 98–100; of author, 100–102
Despair, from sin, 10, 22–23
Determinism, 78–79
Diagnostic descriptions, 56
Dickinson, Emily, 49
Dissociative identity disorder, 61
Divorce, 103
"Do Not Despair" (Benson), 108
Dreams, 53–54, 111–12

Effort, to heal, 46
Eli, 31–32
Eliphaz, 27

Elkanah, 30, 31, 32
Ellis, Albert, 23
Enoch, 19–20
Evans, Richard L., 84
Existential therapy, 90
Extremes, 8
Eyring, Henry B., 28

Faith: reason and, 6–11; of potential therapists, 84–85; in fighting mental illness, 91
Fall, 5–6
False revelations, 54
Family systems therapy, 90
Fasting, 41–42
Faust, James E., 27
Fear, 35
Frances, Allen, 17–18
Frankl, Viktor, 90
Freud, Sigmund, 73
Fundamentalism, 9

Gay individuals, 69–70
Generalized anxiety order, 49
Glasser, William, 90
God: sorrow felt by, 19–20; righteousness of, 44; communication methods of, 53–54; characteristics, perfections, and attributes of, 70–73; body of, 80; covenant relationship with, 97–98
Gottman, John, 29–30
Gottman, Julie, 29–30
Grace, 37–38, 43–48
Greenspan, Miriam, 102

Hannah, 30–33
Healing, 91–92; through Atonement, 24–26, 93–97; through grace of Christ, 37–38; without effort, 46; psychological, medical, and spiritual, 81–82; through spiritual- and religious-oriented psychotherapies, 93–94; examples of, 94–109. *See also* Treating mental illness

INDEX

Heavenly Mother, 72–73, 126n24
Hinckley, Gordon B., 93, 126n24
Holland, Jeffrey R.: depression experienced by, 12–13; on correlating sin with sickness, 24; on perfectionism, 42–43; on nature of God, 71–72; on seeking professional help, 82–83
Holy Ghost, 94–96
Horwitz, Allan, 18
Hunter, Howard W., 109

Impressions: responding to, 57–58; and dealing with depression, 59–60. *See also* Inspiration; Revelation
Indeterminism, 78–79
Infertility, 30–33
Inspiration, 7. *See also* Impressions; Revelation
Instant gratification, 33
Intellectualism, 9–10
"In the Wilderness," 97
Isackson, Darla, 42

Jesus Christ: sorrow felt by, 17; suffering of, 24; healing through, 37–38, 92–93; grace of, 43–48; resurrection of, 80; building foundation upon, 104–5, 106–9; knowing and trusting, 113. *See also* Atonement
Job, 26–27, 28–29
Johnson, Jane Clayson, 29
Joseph Smith Translation, 101
Joy, 19, 20
Judd, Daniel K, 100–102
Judd, Kaye, 112–13
Judging others, 27–28, 76–77
Justice, 68–69

Kimball, Heber C., 71
Korihor, 46–47

Labels, 56
Laws, bounds and, 77

Legalism, 39–42, 47
Lewis C. S., 7
LGBTQ+ individuals, 69–70
Loss, 33
Luther, Martin, 38–42, 43–44, 45

Mania, 19, 20
Martha, 101–102
Matthews, Robert J., 66–67
Maxwell, Neal A., 76, 105–6
McGlashan, Thomas, 62
Medical healing, 81–82
Medication, 35–36, 81, 83, 87–89, 96, 100
Mental health: relationship between religious belief and practice and, 3–5, 52–53, 54–55; research on grace and, 47–48
Mental illness: increase in, 1; causes of, 1–2, 10, 88, 128n32. *See also* Treating mental illness
Mercy, 68–69
Millet, Robert L., 47, 98–100
Miscarriage, 59
Missionary work, anxiety in, 36–38
Monson, Thomas S., 76
Morrison, Alexander B., 83, 87–88
Mortality, sadness, disappointment, and failure as part of, 33
Mother in Heaven, 72–73, 126n24
Multiple personality disorder, 61
Mutism, selective, 48
Mysticism, 9

Nehor, 46
Nelson, Russell M., 6, 7, 19, 40
"Nervous prostration," 15

Oaks, Dallin H., 72; on parenting, 67, 68; on laws and bounds, 77; on enabling power of Atonement, 82; on faith in fighting mental illness, 91
Obedience: obsessive, 38–42;

INDEX

salvation through, 44–45; forced, 66–67
Opposites, counterfeit, 7–11
Overzealousness, 38–42

Packer, Boyd K.: on extremes, 8; on spiritual pain, 23; on healing through Atonement, 25–26; on punishment by sin, 29; on human experience, 33; on doctrine and behavior, 102
Panic attacks, 35
Panic disorder, 49
Parenting: authoritarian, 65–68, 69; permissive, 67, 68, 69; styles of, 67–69; authoritative, 68; supportive, 68–69; and suicide risk, 69–70; and God's characteristics, perfections, and attributes, 70–73
Peace, through Atonement, 44
Peninnah, 30
Perfection, of God, 71
Perfectionism, 42–43
Permissive parenting, 67, 68, 69
Personal responsibility, accepting, 29–30
Personal revelation, 7
Person-centered therapy, 90
Phobias, 49
Plato, 80
Pleasantness, of God, 71
Praise, 29–30
Prayer, 42, 53, 85
Promptings. *See* Impressions; Inspiration; Revelation
Psychological healing, 81–82
Psychotherapy, 82–87, 89–91, 93–94
Psychotic disorders, 52–56; and self-deception, 56–61; schizophrenia, 61–64

Reality therapy, 90
Reason, faith and, 6–11
Redemption, 45–46
Religious belief and practice: relationship between mental health and, 3–5, 52–53, 54–55; science and, 6
Religious-oriented psychotherapies, 93–94
Responsibility, accepting, 29–30
Resurrection, 80
Revelation, 7, 53–54. *See also* Impressions; Inspiration
Rice, Richard, 70
Richards, P. Scott, 93
Righteousness, of God, 44
Riley, Isaac Woodbridge, 52
Rogers, Carl, 90
Russell, Bertrand, 10

Sadness, 17–18, 20. *See also* Depression; Sorrow
Salvation: through Atonement, 44; false teachings on, 46–47; and war in heaven, 66–67
Samuel, 32
Satan: and counterfeit opposites, 7–8, 10–11; and war in heaven, 66–67
Schizophrenia, 61–64
Science, religion and, 6
Scientism, 9–10
Scrupulosity, 36–38
Sears, Heber J., 13–15
Selective mutism, 48
Self-deception, 56–61
Separation anxiety disorder, 48, 49–50
Sickness, correlation of sin with, 23–24
Sin: despair from, 10, 22–23; correlation of sickness with, 23–24; depression and, 23–26; punishment by, 29; scrupulosity and, 36–37; confessing, 41; and self-deception, 57; suffering caused by, 82
Skinner, B. F., 89
Smith, George Albert, 13–17, 75–76
Smith, John Henry, 13, 15–16

INDEX

Smith, Joseph: on extremes, 8; psychological study of, 52; on false revelations, 54; on potential of spirits, 56; on understanding God, 70–71
Smith, Joseph F., 10–11
Snow, Erastus, 72
Social anxiety disorder, 49
Sorrow: felt by Jesus Christ, 17; depression versus, 17–19, 20; felt by God, 19–20
Spirit(s): potential of, 56; body and, 80
Spiritual healing, 81–82
Spiritual manifestations, false, 54
Spiritual-oriented psychotherapies, 93–94
Suffering, 24, 113
Suicide, 69–70, 75–76, 103
Supportive parenting, 68–69

Taylor, Barbara Brown, 27
Temple, 95, 96, 97
Therapist, choosing, 82–83, 84–87
Therapy, 82–87, 89–91, 93–94
Treating mental illness: with medication, 35–36, 81, 83, 87–89, 100; through counseling and therapy, 82–87; theories of, 89–91. *See also* Healing
Truth, and counterfeit, 7–11

Uchtdorf, Dieter F., 27–28, 44–45
Uriah, 22
Uselessness, feelings of, 21

Victim blaming, 26, 27–28, 29
Visions, 53. *See also* Dreams

Wakefield, Jerome, 18
War in heaven, 65–67
Warner, C. Terry, 57–58
Whitney, Orson F., 111
Woodruff, Owen, 112
Works, salvation through, 47
Worthlessness, feelings of, 21

Young, Steve, 49–51
Young adult children, 67